Learning and Writing in Counselling

PROFESSIONAL SKILLS FOR COUNSELLORS

The *Professional Skills for Counsellors* series, edited by Colin Feltham, covers the practical, technical and professional skills and knowledge which trainee and practising counsellors need to improve their competence in key areas of therapeutic practice.

Titles in the series include:

Medical and Psychiatric Issues for Counsellors
Brian Daines, Linda Gask and Tim Usherwood

Personal and Professional Development for Counsellors
Paul Wilkins

Counselling by Telephone
Maxine Rosenfield

Time-Limited Counselling
Colin Feltham

Client Assessment
Stephen Palmer and Gladeana McMahon (eds)

Counselling, Psychotherapy and the Law
Peter Jenkins

Contracts in Counselling
Charlotte Sills (ed.)

Counselling Difficult Clients
Kingsley Norton and Gill McGauley

Learning and Writing in Counselling

Mhairi MacMillan and Dot Clark

SAGE Publications
London • Thousand Oaks • New Delhi

SAGE Publications Ltd
6 Bonhill Street
London EC2A 4PU

SAGE Publications Inc.
2455 Teller Road
Thousand Oaks, California 91320

SAGE Publications India Pvt Ltd
32, M-Block Market
Greater Kailash – I
New Delhi 110 048

British Library Cataloguing in Publication data

A catalogue record for this book is available
from the British Library

ISBN 0 7619 5062 1
ISBN 0 7619 5063 X (pbk)

Library of Congress catalog card number 97–062253

Typeset by Mayhew Typesetting, Rhayader, Powys
Printed in Great Britain by Biddles Ltd, Guildford, Surrey

Contents

Introduction

A student on a counselling skills module, when faced with the requirements for the written assignment, said, in some despair, 'But what is four thousand words *like?*'. In this, she summed up very well the problem that can face those who are coming back into education after a long time, or who have never before written a piece that is four thousand words long. It is not possible to imagine the extent of the task until the task itself has been experienced. Thus to embark on the first written assignment may feel like jumping into the unknown.

This book aims to be a companion and guide not only to those who are about to enter counselling training and to trainees as they go through the course, but also to counselling practitioners who wish to develop their writing skills. We have entitled the book 'Learning and Writing' because we believe that writing can be used to help learning to take place as well as to communicate what has been learned. Indeed, it has been argued that the invention of an alphabetic writing script actually affected the modes of cognition – the ways in which people think – from Greece throughout western Europe (Havelock, 1986: 98–116). Furthermore, 'writing is also claimed to have been an essential force in the emergence of an autonomous psyche making up the inner world of human beings' (Narasimhan, 1991: 177). It is cautioned, however, that this claim may not be valid in the same way for cultures other than European which also have a long history of literature texts, for example, India with the Vedas. In any case, the point we would make is that writing is not something outside of ourselves, that we simply 'do' but something that can affect us inwardly (our way of thinking and our feelings, for example) as well.

More people than ever before are now undertaking training in counselling or counselling skills at various levels. Many of these trainees have been away from formal study for a long time or have never considered themselves academically minded. Others are more used to the demands of higher education – and may be familiar with what four thousand words is like – but not the particular skills of writing about counselling, which must combine theory, practice and personal experience in the proper proportions.

Publications in the field of counselling are burgeoning, too. Counsellors with some experience are increasingly communicating their reflections on that experience to a readership consisting of their peers, counsellors in training and interested lay people. Becoming a 'reflective practitioner' is supported and encouraged by reading what others have written about counselling, and distilling what we read along with our own experience through our own writing about practice.

Yet many will have already realised how large is the gap between the intention to write and actually getting what we want to say down on paper. The ideas are clear, interesting and articulate inside one's head, but stubbornly refuse to emerge on to paper or the word processor in a form that is understandable, grammatical and concise. (The last sentence was amended several times before it was considered satisfactory.) It is important to mention the *frustrating* aspects of writing at the beginning in the hope that they will come as less of an unpleasant surprise and more as simply something that can be accepted and worked through.

On the other hand (mercifully), writing can also be exciting, interesting and even compelling. George Mackay Brown, the Orkney poet and writer, was talking of writing fiction when he said, 'I like the feeling of a blank sheet of paper, an undiscovered country in front of you' (BBC Scotland, 1991) but this sense of adventure and enticement can be felt even when the topic is an assignment task and the sheet of paper is replaced by a computer screen. It can be hard not to let the compulsory nature of writing tasks on a counselling course overshadow any sense of excitement in writing. Yet if that adventurous energy can be held on to, even to a minimal degree, it helps greatly in getting the task done.

Part of our purpose in writing this book is to provide further supportive suggestions and advice that can supplement, and at times stand in for, your own inclination to complete the task. To paraphrase a well-known saying: 'Writing is ten per cent inspiration and ninety per cent perspiration.' Without 'inspiration' a piece of writing has no life or interest, without 'perspiration', the writing does not appear at all.

The book itself is in three parts:

Part I, 'Learning', consists of five chapters which take the reader from before the start of the training course to the consideration of learning skills, methods and approaches. Chapters 1 and 2 consider motivation for training, choice of course, contexts for learning, doubts and anxieties. Chapter 3 looks at a 'body of knowledge' and how it is derived. Chapter 4 focuses on skills and how they are acquired and Chapter 5 explores experiential learning, which has a more or less central place in counselling education.

Part II, 'Communicating Learning', considers and discusses (in eight chapters) the requirements of the course: what trainee counsellors must learn and how that learning can be communicated, principally in the form of written assignments. In this part, we look at some detailed suggestions for getting the work done. Chapter 6 looks at the process of writing as communication and as a learning tool. Chapter 7 deals with assessment procedures that may be encountered on a training course, and gives advice on what information you should get from the course organisers. Chapter 8 gets down to some basic foundations of writing, while Chapter 9 discusses the form of writing – what is acceptable, elegant and readable. In Chapter 10, we look at the important area of reading and how the use that you make of reading material is correctly acknowledged in your own writing. Chapters 11 and 12 focus on problems and difficulties in writing and ways of tackling them as well as locating them within the wider frame of a creative process. Chapter 13 looks at writing about practice from both practical and ethical viewpoints.

Part III, 'Continuing to Learn and to Write', considers what part reading and writing play in the continuing development of a counsellor even after the counselling course is finished. Chapter 14 looks at reading in a wider context and introduces the ideas of narrative and text as constructed in social and cultural contexts. Chapter 15 focuses on writing after the course is complete: reports, reviews, research, conference papers and articles for journals. The last chapter, 16, relates something of our experience in writing this book. We try to 'tell it like it was' as far as possible. It is our hope that this will encourage you, the readers, to try your own hands at writing even when it is no longer obligatory.

So, what *is* four thousand words like? Partial answers to this question can be given in terms of a quantity of pages (between sixteen and twenty longhand A4 pages or thirteen double-spaced pages on the wordprocessor), a length of time (a solid week's work or work spread out over a month), the amount of reading that would go into it and so on. Four thousand words is about the size of many book chapters (Chapter 15, for instance). Of course, only the experience of writing four thousand words will tell you what it is like. And that experience may be different each time.

Here is an analogy from hillwalking. In order to navigate accurately when walking in the Scottish hills (in Scottish weather!) it is essential to know what five hundred metres, say, is like for the one who is the walker. If you have discovered that you take sixty-two double paces to cover one hundred metres of level ground, you have a quite precise knowledge of what five hundred metres would be like. But this changes over rough moorland, for instance (up to sixty-five paces per hundred metres). In terms of time, five hundred metres takes six minutes walking at five kilometres per hour. However, another minute may have to be added for every ten-metre contour climbed in the five hundred metres, more if the walker is tired, and so on. As the hillwalker becomes more experienced, and if she has learned to read a map, she can time herself fairly accurately and know where she is even if the cloud is swirling around her knees. And, of course, each individual walker (or writer) has her or his own pace and characteristics which must be discovered or recognised.

This book aims to accompany you in your discovery of your own learning and writing skills. We hope that it will act as a map of the territory. We offer some fundamental information about how to go about the learning and writing tasks, and pointers to where further help can be found. Nevertheless, you remain the best authority on your own learning and the context in which it takes place. No one has the potential to know you better than you yourself and no one knows your life situation better than you. And from time to time you may need to talk over any difficulties with appropriate people near you – course tutors, for example, or counsellors in the college counselling service or colleagues on the course. With that proviso, we hope that this book will prove to be a useful and valued companion to your learning and writing endeavours, before, during and after your counselling training and that it will aid in developing your skills as a reflective practitioner.

Part I

Learning

1

At the Beginning

People come into counselling training from a wide variety of backgrounds. Some of the more academic of these have been ecology, English literature, social anthropology, theology, drama, psychology, education and philosophy (Thorne and Dryden, 1993). Others have little or no academic training, yet may have lots of practical experience and a real flair for counselling. Some will have had experience of counselling in a voluntary capacity with an agency and will have undergone the agency's training programme. Such programmes can be quite intensive but are unlikely to include much formal written work. Nevertheless, this experience may provide a foretaste of what is to come in a formal training course. People in any of the above groups may also have experienced being a *client* in counselling or psychotherapy.

Whatever your previous history, once you have been accepted on to a counselling training course you may well be wondering what you have let yourself in for. A strange new environment and an unknown future can evoke anxious feelings. Apprehension about the academic aspects of the course may include some worries about being able to complete the required work. Submitting your work for assessment may feel to you as if you are putting yourself on the line to be judged by others. Furthermore, 'academic' work on a counselling course is not wholly objective or impersonal. You need to be prepared to write about your personal feelings and experiences as well as demonstrate understanding of counselling theory. Your practical skills are going to be assessed, too.

If it all seems a bit too strange and daunting, consider taking a course at a very introductory level. For a modest investment of time, effort and money, you can get a taste of what is involved in counselling or in using counselling skills and become clearer about

whether counselling training is for you or not. Local further education evening courses or university continuing education classes
are possible sources of low-cost introductions to counselling. Even
if you do not go on to take counselling training, you may be a better
informed consumer of counselling services as a result of the course.

Type and educational level of course

(1) Introductory courses: usually require only that the applicant
be interested in the subject. They are unlikely to require any written
assignment and do not usually offer any qualification, although
they could in some way count towards Accreditation of Prior
Learning (APL).

(2) Certificate courses in counselling, counselling skills, counselling approaches, counselling theory, counselling practice (and so
on) do not give a training to professional counsellor level. They
may, however, be a useful first step towards entry to such a course.

(3) Diploma in counselling courses usually give a professional
counsellor training. Check this out, however, as different levels of
courses may have the same name (yes, it is confusing). A good
guide is if the course is accredited by the British Association for
Counselling or a similar professional body and/or is academically
validated by a reputable educational institution (university, college
etc.).

(4) Post-graduate-level courses are likely to require a more
academic approach to reading, written work and so on. They do
not necessarily give a better training, either in counselling or
counselling skills, but may be the right choice for those who are
interested in a more theoretical approach and an academic qualification. A post-graduate diploma may also be required for entry to
a Master's degree in counselling studies.

Applying for a place on a course

The first writing task you may be faced with is that of applying for a
place on a course. This is likely to involve completing an application form. Few people like filling in forms and this one in
particular may arouse apprehension. Some personal statements are
likely to be required, in relation to your own life and experience
and why you wish to train in counselling. There will almost
certainly be an element of competition and you will want to give

what are considered to be 'the right answers'. Of course, it is not a matter of finding the right answers, but it is important not to waste your effort applying for courses that are not right for you – whether because of an inappropriate educational level or because you do not feel at home with the course ethos and orientation.

Courses at certificate level do not usually require an application in depth. Some indication of your previous educational experience will be asked for, but even if you have no formal qualifications, do not give up – Accreditation of Prior Experiential Learning (APEL) may be granted (see Chapter 2). There are also courses which do not require formal qualifications for entry.

More will be asked for when applying for a diploma-level course. Here are headings from some application forms for diploma courses (omitting specific details such as address, education, etc).

course 1: *For a course in humanistic counselling*
Relevant work or voluntary experience
Reasons why you have applied for this course

course 2: *For a 'broadly humanistic' training course in counselling*
Describe yourself as you are now
Indicate the significant stages in your development
Indicate where you see yourself going
Make three statements about how you see the nature and purpose of counselling

Each of these sections is given about half of an A4 page for response.

course 3: *For a training course in a psychodynamic approach*
A 500-word personal statement
Current work and personal situation including any counselling work you are doing
Previous counselling courses attended (if any)
Any information you feel is relevant to this application
Why do you wish to join this course?
How did you hear about this course?

course 4: *For a training course in the person-centred approach*
Your present opportunities for practising as a counsellor (if you do not have current opportunities for practice, please give details of your plans for any

such opportunities and describe any earlier practice opportunities you may have had)

Your present strengths and weaknesses in the role of helper

Your reasons for wanting to embark on this course at this time in your life

Please go into detail on the ways in which the Person-Centred Approach, as you currently understand it, relates to your own personality and experience. Do not hesitate to comment on the 'conflict' as well as the 'fit'

Your thoughts about the financial and time commitments of the course in relation to your current life

What makes you confident that you can handle the theoretical parts of the course including the reading and the written assignments? (Applicants will vary in their prior educational experience – rather than ask for specific previous attainments we prefer to consider the applicant as an individual whose confidence in this area may be derived from various prior experiences)

Please write here anything else you would want us to know about you

course 5:   *For an integrative course in counselling*

Pro-forma details of education and training (from 11 years old!), counselling courses attended, counselling experience, current employment, plus –

1,000-word letter of application presenting your theoretical approach to counselling

Explain the basic principles of this approach and relate it to your counselling practice, with reference to the appropriate literature

Give your reasons for wishing to take the course and what attracts you about the programme

You can see that there is a great variation in the amount and nature of the information that an application form requires. Courses 1, 2, 4 and 5 are in Higher Education Institutions, course 3 is moving toward academic accreditation by a university. Course 4 is alone in this group in asking explicitly about your estimation of your ability to handle the academic part of the work on the course, although the long letter required by course 5 may be intended (at least in part) to enable course staff to judge your academic ability. The other courses also may make some inferences about your writing ability from the way you complete your application.

Completing the diploma application form

Perhaps it should go without saying, but we stress the rule of being honest in any application you make for counselling training. Apart from the riskiness of making false statements or exaggerated claims, it is entirely against the ethos of counselling itself. Nevertheless, it makes sense to be selective – course staff do not want to spend time reading irrelevant material when they have a large number of applications to process – and to present yourself and your experience clearly and in a good light.

Consider all your experience in connection with other people where interpersonal skills were required. This does not only apply to counselling or obvious counselling skills contexts. A person who works in a bank (for example) may well have listened to people in emotional turmoil, and have been able to appreciate the value of attentive listening, clear information giving and understanding the client's 'frame of reference'. Here are some other points that are worth thinking about before completing your application:

- Reading – what kind of books interest you? Which books about counselling? Are you familiar with theoretical texts? Which counselling approaches? What other non-fiction do you read? Which fiction interests you? (See also Chapter 14.)
- Writing – have you done any writing that might be useful in terms of practice? Kept a journal? What writing tasks have you undertaken in formal education – essays, dissertations, reports, poetry?
- Motivation for counselling – who am I? What do I have to offer other people? What do I need from others? What do I believe is most helpful for other people? What has been most helpful for me?

Autobiography

Some courses ask applicants for an autobiographical account. This should trace your involvement with change, transitions, life events and their aftermath. It may also include reflections on patterns in your life and discussion of any counselling you have yourself undertaken, as well as personal development leading to increase in your self-awareness. This is also an opportunity to examine your beliefs and system of values, the view you take of yourself, fellow humans and the environment. You may also include your own ideas about how people change and how such change can be encouraged.

Whatever the theoretical approach, the work of counselling involves the use of your self. A counselling training course, there-fore, is an opportunity to learn about yourself. An autobiographical exercise is useful not only for reflecting on your life so far, but also for considering the questions: what am I doing here? why coun-selling training? why now? why this course?

Life events

Try the exercise of noting down some of the important events in your life. Then see if there is any thread running through that tended to lead you towards a training in counselling.

The decision to embark on a counselling course (especially, but not only, if it is full-time) may cause considerable disruption in a person's life. Such a decision may also *follow* a period of upheaval or a major life transition or it may be as a result of a cumulative experience of life changes. The following extract illustrates the last of these:

> Rather than look at my life events chronologically, I decided to look at major influences. Then I realised that these influences have obviously meant changes for me which have involved loss. I guess the main theme of my life has been a series of losses. On reflection, I realise that I see life itself as a series of losses and changes which one needs to adjust to, or at least learn to adjust to in order to survive healthily.
> (Dorothy Degenhart, 1994)

Motivation

Clearly, something has motivated you to reach this point. Writing an autobiographical review helps clarify the dynamic processes which have moved (or pushed or directed) you, gently or urgently, to the point of deciding to train in counselling. This is what motivation consists of; it is defined in the dictionary as 'that which incites to action; inner impulse'.

The movement implicit in 'motivation' may be both 'towards' and 'away from'. For one of the authors, her movement was away from working in school teaching (and the kind of interpersonal relating dominant in that environment) and towards a different kind of interpersonal relating. This she found firstly in large group workshops which later led her to a training course in counselling (MacMillan, 1993).

Sometimes in the middle of a training course, when the going may become difficult and progress is hard to make, students may wonder what on earth possessed them to start on this venture. They may even consider leaving. It can be useful, then, to take time to recall the motivation for taking the course in the first place. Look at it again: What moved you to come here? What aspirations did you want to fulfil? What in your life did you wish or need to move away from? Can the impulse that brought you here still help you to keep going?

Commitment

Taking time to recall and renew one's motivation is part of one's *commitment* to completing the course. It is unlikely that such a commitment would be made without careful consideration followed by a conscious decision to carry it through. It is possible that a person might drift into a counselling skills level course, especially if it were a modular one, with open entry to the first module. Entering on a diploma course, however, which normally involves an interview and detailed application, will already have required a degree of commitment. During the selection process, course staff should check carefully that applicants know the extent of the commitment they are undertaking (see Purton, 1991: 34).

Sustaining and fulfilling the initial commitment depends on qualities of perseverance and stamina. Commitment may need to be supported by strategies for avoiding procrastination (putting work off till 'tomorrow') and the development of constructive study methods. All of this can be viewed as part of one's personal development throughout the course which adds to one's learning about learning. This learning has even been considered to be the most significant kind:

Assessing how I learn and how I provide evidence of what I learn is really more fundamental than assessing what I have learned. (Heron, 1988 cited in Connor, 1994: 164)

An increased understanding of the process of learning may also be useful in helping clients, not only for counsellors working in educational settings but because counselling is itself, in large part, an educational process. (MacMillan, 1993)

Your commitment to yourself to complete the course should include promising yourself that you will ask for help when you need it. The course organisers, tutors and fellow students are all potential sources of support and help. A further possibility might be to have some counselling for yourself. If the training course is located within an educational institution, there is likely to be a counselling service which you can use. Check out beforehand whether students in training on your course undertake placements in the student counselling service, as you may prefer not to meet your fellow trainees when going to counselling. For that reason, some Higher Education Institutions do not accept trainees for placement in their own counselling service.

Context for learning

There are many different contexts for the provision of counselling training. The actual context of your course will affect the kind of learning experience you may expect. The course may be full- or part-time; it may be modular or not. You may remain with the same group (cohort) of trainees – if the course is of diploma level this is more likely – or be part of a different group for each module. Some modular courses offer great flexibility over timing and may attract people who continue in full-time employment if, for example, it takes place mainly at weekends.

A full-time course implies a greater degree of disruption to normal life, compared to a part-time course. One of the authors moved household, children and all, to a city three hundred miles away for the year's duration of the course. This makes it more likely that the closeness of the group and intensity of the training experience are increased.

Your choice of course may well be linked to practical considera- tions in your current life situation. There are now many counselling training courses to choose from. Funding remains difficult, unless you can fund yourself or are lucky enough to be funded by, for example, your employer. In any case, reflecting right at the start on what is your purpose in taking this training and how you are making some important choices may help you find solid ground on which to start. If, on the other hand, there are many aspects of the choice of course that you are unclear about, you may realise that now is not the right time to undertake counselling training.

Key point

However much you have wanted to take a counselling training course and however hard you have worked to be accepted on one, you may still feel bewildered and dismayed by the academic requirements of the course, and be anxious about whether you can successfully complete the assignments. Taking time and care to complete the application helps you and the course staff decide if this training is right for you.

2

The Training Course

There are many reasons why a particular course in counselling is chosen. Often these are pragmatic, such as that a course is geographically convenient, or that the structure fits the applicant's time schedule (i.e. full-time, part-time, modular, etc.) People who live in areas where there are a lot of courses on offer will have more choice in this respect. Two other characteristics of courses have implications for learning issues and writing skills needed. These are (1) educational level of the course and (2) the theoretical model or orientation of the course.

The educational level of the course

Courses are offered at a wide range of levels, for example:

(a) Short exploratory courses, 10–40 hours, often over one or two weekends, useful for finding out if you are seriously interested in counselling.
(b) Introductory courses in counselling skills, in a wide range of counselling approaches.
(c) Post-graduate-level courses leading to a Certificate in Counselling Skills/Approaches. There are also some undergraduate certificate courses.
(d) Undergraduate and post-graduate Diploma in Counselling courses – this is the most usual form for a professional level training in counselling.
(e) Master's Degree courses in counselling psychology/counselling studies and related subjects, the exact specification depending on the nature of the institution offering the course. A number of higher education institutions (in Scotland, for instance) have a Modular Master's Degree scheme, in which modules are taken

in order to build up from Certificate, through Diploma to Master's level.

There is some evidence that counsellor training is moving towards post-graduate standards. This may well be in order to provide a more professionally credible status, in line with the aspirations of the United Kingdom Council for Psychotherapy and the British Psychological Society.

The number and nature of training courses 'on the market' are changing all the time. Looking through the pages of *Counselling – The Journal of the British Association for Counselling*, for example, you will find many courses on offer. Many of these courses, and almost all of those listed from (c) to (e) are located in or accredited by Higher Education Institutions and have academic entrance requirements appropriate to the institution. Widespread schemes for Accreditation of Prior Learning (APL) and Accreditation of Prior Experiential Learning (APEL) mean that applicants without formal academic qualifications are unlikely to be turned down on those grounds. However, it does mean, especially at post-graduate level, that these courses will expect a certain standard of academic writing in the completion of course assignments – even though it has been pointed out that there is no evidence that people who write better essays make better counsellors!

Context or setting

Clues to some of the other characteristics of a course can be inferred from the setting in which the course is based. Examples of different settings are: a former teacher-training college, now an institute of education within a university; an independent counselling unit within the faculty of education of a university; attachment to a psychology department in a university; a university department of adult education; a university department of theology; a pastoral organisation; a private training consultancy; a professional organisation of psychotherapists, and so on.

It is worthwhile to ask the staff of the training organisation some pertinent questions about its background, characteristics of their students (work settings, full- or part-time, proportion of male to female) as well as about the ethos of the organisation and its value and belief system. This makes it more likely that it will fit you as a person and your training needs.

Accreditation of Prior Learning

It is important, too, to find out what arrangements the course or institution has in place for the accreditation of any previous training or learning you have undertaken towards fulfilling the course requirements. If a certificate or other paper qualification has been awarded and if it can be shown that the standard of the previous course is as high as the current one (not necessarily an easy process) then APL can be a relatively straightforward procedure.

Accreditation of Prior Experiential Learning (APEL) is an allied mechanism for assessing the academic standing of those without formal qualifications. The procedure by which it is assessed may be extensive and detailed or more informal. It can be used both when applying for entry to a course and when applying for credit to be given for a part of the course syllabus or a module. In the first case, you may be asked to write about your counselling work to date as well as an autobiographical account of life experience and reasons for applying to join the course. In the second case you may be asked to describe the relevant experience and also to complete any written assignment for that part of the course. Procedures vary from one institution to another, so always ask for specific details.

At this point you may ask: 'Is applying for APL worth my while?' In fact, the work needed to go through a rigorous procedure may convince an applicant that it would be as convenient to take the whole course in the first place. On the other hand, you can save both time and money by not doing the same work all over again.

The disadvantages of using Accreditation of Prior Learning, in whatever form, are set out in Dryden, Horton and Mearns (1995) and centre round the threats to 'cohort integrity' and 'course identity' and thus, in effect, to the most facilitative learning environment.

Credit accumulation and transfer

Accreditation of Prior Learning is in some ways facilitated by the Credit Accumulation Transfer Scheme (CATS). This is not confined to counsellor training but is operative throughout higher education. Each module on a course is assigned a specific number of

CATS points (or in Scotland, ScotCAT points) which, in theory, can be transferred to another institution as part credit towards the requirements for the institution's course. Therefore, many institutions now indicate the number of 'points' that are awarded for successful completion of its training courses (in some cases, for individual modules). For example an introduction to counselling course may carry '20 CATS points at level 1' and a certificate in psychodynamic counselling '90 CATS points at level 1'. In Scotland, an example would be of a post-graduate diploma with each module rated at 15 ScotCAT points at Scottish Master's (SM) level (90 ScotCAT points overall).

As this can be confusing, ask the staff of the institution concerned what the rating is for the courses or modules that you are interested in and at what point it is permissible to transfer into a particular course. This last is important since many (perhaps most) counsellor training courses wish to preserve the integrity of the course cohort. This means that it is unlikely to be possible to join such a course in the middle even if it is of modular construction.

Vocational qualifications (NVQs and SVQs)

National Vocational Qualifications (in Scotland, Scottish Vocational Qualifications) are being developed following government initiatives in education and training. They are intended to fill a vocational gap between school and academic qualifications. The Advice, Guidance and Counselling Lead Body has been working since 1992 to develop a nationally recognised structure for standards and competencies in this field. More recently, 'psychotherapy' competencies have been added.

In this scheme, much of what has been regarded as 'skills' training is translated into 'competency based' training and assessment. In order to do this, the competencies of counselling and psychotherapy have been broken down into their constituent parts. A summary list of 'Tasks, Skills and Competencies' is given by Inskipp (1996: 6–8). Inskipp and Wheeler (1996) are useful sources for information about NVQs, which, however, have yet to be finalised.

In Scotland, SVQs will replace the ScotVEC (Scottish Vocational Education Council) modules. At the time of writing, some Introduction to Counselling and Certificate in Counselling courses are designated as ScotVEC modules.

Theoretical model or orientation

Some, perhaps the majority of courses offer training in one specific counselling approach or theoretical orientation. The growth in the number of such courses may well be connected with the expansion of the BAC's scheme for the accreditation of training courses (formerly known as 'course recognition'), which does not, at present, accredit courses 'which encourage students to develop their own eclectic or integrative models' unless they are presented within a 'core integrative framework' (Dryden, Horton and Mearns, 1995).

The core theoretical model chosen for the course has implications for the content of what has to be learned, the shape of the learning process and the assessment procedures. Below are examples of three of the main models of counselling offered in educational institutions.

Psychodynamic

The psychodynamic approach is underpinned by a wealth of theory. Courses based on it look for understanding of a considerable 'body of knowledge', and a fair degree of literacy skill may be required to describe and discuss theoretical concepts. There is a strong emphasis on unconscious processes; thus, the way in which trainees handle deadlines, anxiety and so on are also 'assessed' even if not formally. The very specialised language of psychodynamics must be learned and used appropriately in a way that shows understanding, not mere parroting.

A typical Diploma in Psychodynamic Counselling requires the following written assignments:

a 500-word personal statement on application
a theoretical paper on the basic principles of psychodynamic counselling
a personal journal and training portfolio
a counselling process paper based on clinical work
a process paper illustrating the different theoretical approaches to clinical work
a detailed account of the development and implementation of a project within the community
a further theoretical paper

With a large body of knowledge to be transmitted to students, psychodynamic courses require much reading, retaining and understanding of theory and analysis of clinical material in line with theoretical constructs. Trainees will also be required to undertake extensive personal therapy or counselling.

Person-centred
The person-centred approach has been said to be 'lean on theory' (McLeod and Wheeler, 1995). At any rate, there is less of a body of knowledge to absorb and understand. Concomitant with an emphasis on *experiencing* as the ground of theory, students are expected to integrate theoretical concepts with their own experience. Thus a willingness to disclose personal concerns and to write in a style both personal and theoretically consistent is called upon.

The person-centred approach places a particular value on power-sharing and collaboration (between trainers and trainees as well as between client and counsellor) which usually leads to as much freedom of choice as is consistent with professional standards both as to the content (subject) of assignments and the medium or form in which they are submitted. For example, one person-centred course stipulates that assignments should be 'a meaningful challenge' for individual course members, rather than a blanket assignment, which might have little meaning for some but be fruitful for others. Such a course might be willing to accept audiotaped assignments as well as written. But there remain limits; the submission would need to communicate the trainee's ideas clearly, which would not be true for, say, a painting (unless supported by a verbal commentary) which could only invoke interpretations from its viewers.

A typical Diploma in Person-centred Counselling requires the following written assignments:

an autobiographical statement on application
an essay on the therapeutic conditions
an analysis of a tape of a counselling session
an essay on the person-centred approach compared and contrasted with another approach
a case study
an evaluative self-assessment statement

The dominant mode of learning on person-centred courses will be experiential. This mode is personally involving, self-initiated (or group-initiated), pervasive, evaluated by the learner and its essence is in the personal meaning generated for the learner (Rogers, 1969). However, most person-centred courses still seek to transmit some body of knowledge through direct teaching and required reading and to assess it correspondingly. Such reading would include the seminal works of Carl Rogers (1951, 1961, 1980) and a growing body of contemporary writing e.g. Levant and Shlien (1984), Mearns and Thorne (1988), Combs (1989), Mearns (1995).

Skills-based or eclectic/integrated courses

A significant number of established courses describe their approach as 'eclectic', or more often nowadays, 'integrated' or 'integrative'. The wide variation in eclectic models has been described by, for example, Dryden (1984) and McLeod (1993). Most of the courses that come under this heading are of the 'developmental eclectic' or 'transtheoretical eclectic' variety which have been developed into a number of 'integrative models' (e.g. Connor, 1994). To some extent, the integrative approach is likely to attract those people who are not satisfied that any single theory of counselling can address a full enough range of human psychological difficulties or modes of psychological change. A course may also adopt a 'central unifying concept' (McLeod, 1993: 104) such as the 'relational model' of Holmes, Paul and Pelham (1996). On the other hand, many eclectic/integrative models, including Egan's 'skilled helper' model (Egan, 1993), are primarily informed by a cognitive-behavioural perspective (McLeod, 1993: 104). This in itself may limit the breadth of issues such a model can address.

Considerable emphasis is put on skills training, and to an extent on the 'technical eclecticism' approach which seeks to assess client needs and match them with appropriate interventions by the counsellor (Dryden, 1984; McLeod, 1993). There will be particular focus, then, on assessment of the skills that are appropriate to different stages in the counselling process. However, theory is not neglected and theoretical knowledge is assessed in various ways. A diploma in an integrative approach to counselling might require the following written assignments:

learning journal – weekly A4 page entry, termly summary sheet, yearly personal development profile, 1,500 words   .

group development learning statement, incorporating feedback from facilitator and peers

statement or essay on the nature of the integrative model case study

counselling practice file – preparation for supervision, writing up supervision sessions, framework for reflection

statement on supervision themes, areas for development, implementation of therapeutic strategies, reflective skills

evaluative transcript of videotaped counselling session, evidencing skills of support, challenge, immediacy, resourcefulness, dynamics

research project dissertation (about 10,000 words)

Your response to the course

Most courses have four aspects:

Exploring the theoretical approach
reading, lectures, note-taking, integrating the body of knowledge as personal meaning

Client work and skills practice
identifying and practising skills, feeling de-skilled, giving and receiving feedback
video/audio-tape analysis, using supervision

Personal development
experiential learning in groups, self-concept change, keeping a personal journal, personal therapy

Completing the assignments
organising the work, fulfilling the performance criteria, handling the emotional factors

How do you feel about each of these aspects in turn?
Are any of the above feelings rooted in past educational experiences?
How do you assess your resources to cope with each aspect?
Can you identify aspects of your 'stance' with respect to a preferred model of counselling?
How does your stance fit with the theoretical approach to the course?

Selection

A number of books and articles which critically examine the nature of training courses in counselling are now being published. See, for example Dryden and Feltham (1994), Dryden, Horton and Mearns (1995), Wheeler (1994) and Purton (1991). The last-mentioned article is a very useful (if limited) analysis of the selection and assessment procedures for differently oriented training courses. In it, Purton points out that the differing emphases given to aspects of selection of trainees will also show up in the procedures for assessment. Selection, then, is the very beginning of the entire assessment process of the course.

Check out, therefore, what the selection process will consist of and on what factors emphasis will fall. Consider whether or not you feel comfortable with it. For example, what is the power distribution between applicant and selectors? Is the interview encouraged to be a dialogue? Is there a concern about your own possible psychopathology – or not? Is the emphasis on your awareness of unconscious processes or on your ability to empathise? How is your previous experience of counselling and/or personal development (either as giver or receiver) to be presented, and judged?

In his analysis, Purton sees each course distinguished by 'the kind of fear or concern which predominates'. His views are that on a person-centred course, this is a fear of the abuse of power; on an academic M.Sc. course, it is likely to be fear of bias (lack of 'scientific' objectivity); on a psychosynthesis (transpersonal) course, fear of 'betrayal of the spirit' and on a psychodynamic course the greatest concern is likely to be 'fear of unconscious pathology'. You might find it interesting, should you be invited to a selection interview for counselling training, to ask the interviewer(s) what they see as being the greatest concern or fear manifested on that particular course.

Key Point

The nature and setting of the training course has implications for the kind of learning and writing skills needed as well as *what* is learned and *how* the learning takes place. The 'core theoretical model' of the course should be consistent with its learning approach

---

3

Learning Style in a Learning Community

What would you expect to learn on a counselling training course? This could be summed up as learning about oneself and others, learning the skills of counselling and learning the body of theoretical knowledge associated with that particular counselling approach. The opportunities for learning presented on the course may include lectures, seminars and discussions, structured exercises, unstructured group meetings (large and small), skills practice with feedback and the use of audio and video recording.

In many higher education institutions, seminars and tutorials are small groups, led by a tutor, a member of the academic staff, where ideas are presented and discussed. These ideas may be in the form of papers presented by the students or reading assigned by the tutor and so on. Not all counselling training courses follow this format; it may be considered unnecessarily academic in professional counsellor training. If a seminar system is used, it is of most value when participants feel able to speak out freely and contribute their ideas to the discussion.

Some courses assign a personal tutor to each of the course members. On one course their function is described as: 'to explore with them (i.e. course members) their relationship, personal and professional, to the course as it progresses'. In tutorial meetings, students can review their need for personal support, management of course work and learning in terms of theory, practice and self-evaluation. The tutorial system exists both to support course members and to aid their learning.

Formal learning

The most formal kind of learning on the course is likely to be the learning of theoretical concepts whether from lectures or from reading recommended books and articles. This requires skills such as note-taking, summarising, reading purposefully and searching the literature. This may be the sort of learning that comes closest to your previous educational experiences.

It is worth reflecting on what these previous experiences meant to you and how they affect you now.

- If earlier experiences were unsatisfactory or judgemental, you may be feeling anxious, defensive and unskilled.
- You may switch into 'automatic pilot' and rely on skills which produced results in the past without re-examining and re-evaluating the usefulness of these skills for the present task.
- You may jettison previously acquired skills and try a new approach to learning theory which fits more closely with the chosen counselling approach and your own learning style.

One of the authors found that her attempt to discard formal learning skills from the past was helped by moving away from reading and writing at a table to lying in bed surrounded by a clutter of books, notes, personal journal and packet of biscuits. For another student, the move might be in the opposite direction!

Authority

To reflect on your past educational experience is to pay attention to where you are starting from. In this respect, it is worth thinking about your attitude to authority, for this is likely to connect with the theoretical model of the course you have chosen as well as your own learning style. Oatley (1980: 86) reminds us that one mode of learning is when 'a body of knowledge is passed from experts to students', paralleling the process 'in which history and ways of seeing the world were passed on by elders'.

In learning the theory, you will need to become familiar with the key concepts and assumptions of that approach by, for example, getting to know the work of eminent thinkers, writers and prac-titioners – the 'elders' – within it. How do you respond to the authority of these elders? Do you submit, accept, even idealise? Challenge, criticise, rebel? Feel powerless and overwhelmed? Feel bored, isolated or even alienated? All students have experienced some of these feelings at times in the course of their training – and some students have experienced all of them!

Perhaps your response to traditional authority is influenced by the level of personal commitment you have made to your chosen counselling approach. This choice may go back to your earliest experience of counselling. On the other hand, you may find yourself on a particular course more by accident than design. The intensity of your involvement in the particular counselling model may well affect your willingness to examine critically the model itself and the elders of the tradition. However, the process of examining and questioning the core theoretical model will be crucial to integrating the theory in a way that gives it personal meaning.

What is a theory of counselling?

Counselling theories make assumptions in the following areas (Dryden, 1984):

- view or image of human beings
- concepts of psychological health (and its opposite)
- acquisition and perpetuation of psychological problems
- factors in bringing about psychological (personality) change

Counselling approaches vary in the amount of emphasis put on to each of these areas. For example, psychodynamic approaches have a vast body of theory concerning the links between childhood experience and later dysfunctioning, whereas cognitive-behavioural approaches virtually ignore this topic. For a summary of 'specialisation' in counselling theories, see McLeod (1993: 91).

Another view of 'the desirable characteristics of a trustworthy theory of therapy' is given by Combs (1989: 11). Effective theory, he states, must be:

- comprehensive
- accurate
- as simple and orderly as possible

- internally consistent
- appropriate for problems confronted
- responsive to new information or conditions

Critical analysis

Whatever approach to counselling you prefer, it is essential to be prepared to think critically about its theoretical model. The list of 'desirable characteristics' given by Combs (above) is one possible framework for your analysis. Other frameworks are given by, for example, Dryden (1984), McLeod (1993), Nelson-Jones (1984). It may help to clarify the different levels of analysis of counselling theory to ask yourself these questions:

What are the salient features of this particular theory of counselling?

How do these features fit the framework given by, say, Dryden in his 'comparative analysis' of individual therapies (Dryden, 1984: 295–310)?

What are your own critical thoughts on the theoretical model and how it fits (or does not fit) your own practice?

Learning style

Each of us has our own individual learning style. On a counselling training course, that personal learning style will be located within a learning community made up of the other students, tutors, practice supervisors and so on. The broader learning community might even be considered to be the exponents of counselling whom we can contact through reading their writing (articles and books), viewing and discussing videos and by taking part in conferences.

It makes sense to consider how your personal style fits with the learning approach favoured by the course. Of course, your learning style may change over the years. Both authors of this book have an academic background (Scottish secondary education, universities and higher degrees) but for one of us at least, entering the path of counselling studies coincided with a marked change in learning style. This came about through her participation in intensive group workshops, giving experience of the person-centred approach and the influence of Carl Rogers, and not opening a book of his until several years later (MacMillan, 1993).

One general description (Honey and Mumford, 1986) suggests four main learning styles. *Activists*, it is said, involve themselves fully in new experiences – whatever is going on right now – and will try anything once. However, they are liable to get bored with the details of carrying things through. *Reflectors* stand back and consider things carefully; they gather information and weigh it all up before making any decision. They are often observers but leave it as late as possible (sometimes too late) before committing themselves. *Theorists* develop their own theories on the basis of logical principles and reality testing. They can be rather rigid and reject anything that does not fit; thus, they are not good at dealing with ambiguity or 'irrational' feelings. *Pragmatists* want to try out new ideas in practice right away; they like solving problems in a practical way and finding out what works. But they are impatient with talking things through, with 'what if?' attitudes, and with lengthy working out of what might have caused the problem.

This is a fairly crude classification. Nevertheless, it is easy to see how a pragmatist might become impatient with or dismissive of the psychodynamic approach's emphasis on discovering the child-hood origins of psychological difficulty or how a reflector might doubt the value of an approach that seems superficially only to deal with symptoms.

A learning community

The core theoretical model should (according, at least, to the British Association for Counselling) inform every aspect of the course (admission, structure, content, nature of staff involvement, assessment rationale). Therefore, you are being presented with a great deal of material on which to reflect. If the core model is integrated into the fabric of the course, it is central to your experience and not just available in formal theory sessions.

Learning does not take place in isolation from others. To concentrate only on individual learning styles would obscure this fact. At the simplest level, understanding can be shared and developed within the cohort of students through formal and informal discussion, sharing research, literature references and so on. There may also be a more subtle way in which learning is enhanced by the group situation itself. Samuels (1993: 279) writes about the phenomenon of 'shared psychological dynamics that show up in groups'. This phenomenon can also be experienced in shared learning within the learning community.

Being a participant in a group of thirty or more people (although more commonly between twelve and twenty-four members) is not always a pleasant or even comfortable experience. It may feel really terrifying to speak up in such a group, to make a personal statement 'revealing' yourself to others. You may be assuming that these others know more than yourself, whether about the topic being discussed or about the 'rules' of interacting in groups like this one. It is most likely that there are no rules, beyond the ground rules for the group which should be clearly stated at the beginning by the course staff. The question of rules is distinct from the issue of the norms that can build up during the group process. Often a key member of a group is one who is willing to challenge the norms. Whether or not that member receives support within the group may mark a crucial point in the group's functioning. However, many of those who have taken part in groups, whether or not as part of a formal training, will testify to the rewards that can follow when one speaks up in the group, despite the anxiety and sense of risk that may be experienced in doing so. It may be arguable that there is a division in approaches to counsellor training between those who believe that greater value (that is, more learning about self and others) can be gained from, say, two hundred hours of group work than from the same time in individual therapy. Of course, it depends on the quality of the group and the quality of the therapy; neither are these options mutually exclusive.

The sense of 'belonging to a group' has more than one side to it. Some people may well have mixed feelings about being swallowed up by the group, and of having to conform. Indeed, there is a real issue in that 'counselling' has itself become something of a sub-culture in our society, with its own specialised language, value system and world view. Purton (1991: 47–8), in his analysis of four training courses, writes, 'To some extent, counsellor training must involve something of an *initiation into the tradition* which is embodied in the training course' (our italics). This does not seem to leave much room for individual thinking or original contribution to the body of cultural knowledge.

However, traditions and cultures can change and are changed by the individuals within them. The process of counsellor training, or education, like other forms of education is, in part, to do with 'transmitting the culture' (MacMillan, 1993: 131). But that is not the

One trainee's group experience

The beginning

My diary of that first weekend recorded a heightening of some of these fears and anxieties during the very early stages of the group experience. A sharing of backgrounds took place which brought out strong feelings of inferiority in myself. I perceived some people as 'experts', i.e. people who knew a great deal about a subject and because they were already working in counselling set-ups surely had an amazing amount of knowledge and experience that I lacked. I felt the group was almost divided into two, the 'experts' and the rest. I managed to deal with this to some extent by sharing my feelings and anxieties in the small group. By looking at them, acknowledging them and sharing them, I was able to have a sense of not being alone. This brought a great sense of comfort and with it came the realisation that perhaps I may have a distinct advantage over my perceived 'experts' in that my coming on this course with no preconceived theories or historical practices to relate to would not cause me conflict. Being the 'beginner' could possibly have its advantages!

The middle

I am beginning to have a sense of having moved on in my relationships with the group. Although not participating as deeply as some of the others (in the large group) I have accepted that perhaps that is how it is to be for me, and with this recognition, I feel OK. But I also decided to look at why this might be. I was conscious of feelings of envy within myself directed to some of the members, who to my mind seemed able to express themselves very eloquently whilst I was aware that I tended to speak very plainly. One in particular who in the beginning I had labelled as one of the 'experts' . . . was having, on occasion, the effect of silencing me. How could I with my limited counselling and academic background contribute anything worthwhile compared to someone like this? . . . I couldn't quite understand what the problem was because a lot of what she said was very interesting, but when I looked at this more closely I became aware that I was only understanding some of what was being said and this had the effect of disempowering me.

The end

I have been very fortunate to have experienced this amazing feeling of freedom within this small group – a feeling which was unrecognisable when compared to the feelings felt at the beginning of the course. It has brought with it an appreciation of the experience and an understanding of counselling that no amount of reading books could possibly have given me. But the reading of books will always be an important source of information and I am acutely aware that if I wish to continue in the world of counselling, a regular time will have to be set aside for this task. The learning experience does not end with this diploma course! (Leitch, 1997) whole story. The process of education is one of culture *creating* as well as culture *transmitting* (Bruner, 1986). Each of us involved in counselling may make our own contribution to the body of knowledge (for example by engaging in research and by writing) as well as learning from those 'elders' who have written the books and lead the training courses that we undertake.

Being part of a group can be a supportive context for learning but can also encourage comparison with other students who are imagined to be better than oneself – cleverer, more skilful, harder-working. This can set up an emotional barrier to learning, which should be tackled before it interferes with a student's progress. When there is open communication between the members of the whole learning community (students and tutors), then it is easier to defuse fantasies about not being good enough. It is, however, likely to take time for such communication to be established. On the final module of a diploma course on which one of the authors was a tutor, a course member was reflecting that at the start of the course she felt that many of her fellow students 'had such a lot of counselling experience' and she felt inadequate in comparison. Another participant responded, 'Well, M, I always saw *you* as one of the most experienced ones!'

Two further points about the place of group experience in training: the first is to point out that many of the feelings you may be experiencing in the group situation may mirror the feelings that clients experience when they come into counselling – anxiety, embarrassment, shyness, sense of inferiority and so on. The second point is that here is an opportunity to apply some of the theoretical constructs of the core model on the course to helping you resolve your difficult feelings. For example:

- Person-centred: climate of trust engendered by empathic responding, acceptance and congruent relating enable expression of both past and current feelings and exploration of personal meaning.
- Psychodynamic: relating the group experience to patterns within the early family situation; identifying times in the group when the 'basic assumptions' (Bion, 1961) may be operating, i.e. pairing, dependency, fight or flight.
- Rational Emotive Behaviour Therapy: identifying thinking problems, unrealistic personal rules, tackling shyness, for instance, by disputing the underlying beliefs.

■ Transactional Analysis: making a structural analysis of which ego states are operating to produce feelings of shyness, inferiority, etc.; analysing transactions in the group in order to see how communication can be screwed up, perhaps detecting underlying script injunctions and so on.

Creating a 'shared culture' can be a very powerful experience. In the group, as the culture becomes defined, norms, both implicit and explicit, emerge; for example, agreed assumptions such as 'counselling is a good thing'; or 'our "brand" of counselling (psychodynamic/REBT/person-centred/eclectic) is the best'. Norms about members' behaviour in the group are also likely to arise: must not be silent; must cry and/or shout; must not intellectualise; must value skills and theory more than emotional expression – or the other way round. This may engender intense personal investment in the core theoretical model by both course members and staff. It follows that it can be very hard to challenge the norms or question the theory, since to do so feels like risking both individual security and membership of the learning community.

> **I Challenge the Norms (extract from a self-evaluative statement)**
>
> Reading Masson's *Against Therapy* (1989) made me think there is no way of getting the power balance right in therapy, so it is always open to abuse. I sensed in the course that the group had a lot invested in counselling but part of me resisted going along with any group 'belief'. I felt I had to find 'a wee, small fingernail of truth for me – in humility, a little thing that I can go on' (personal journal).
>
> On Friday, the previous day having been spent on 'Social Construction of Reality', I shared how I felt in the community meeting. Looking back, with a bit of distance, I realise I was already learning the value of putting out and owning where I am, but I can hardly communicate the fear, anxiety and loneliness which that meant at the time. Having spent the previous day talking about implicit and explicit norms, my fears picked up on what I felt were the implicit norms held by some of our group – 'she should have sorted herself out before she came on this course', and perceiving me as threatening by questioning the value of counselling.

Group membership

It is not always easy to be part of a group. Indeed the mandatory inclusion of groupwork in counselling training has itself been challenged on the grounds that the authors 'do not believe that a case has been made that groupwork is an essential component of counsellor training' (Irving and Williams, 1996). This is not a view with which we agree, but it is necessary that course tutors have a coherent rationale for the inclusion of groupwork and have themselves extensive experience in groups and knowledge of group dynamics.

One view of group training is that its purpose is 'to help people learn how to learn in the areas of self-understanding and relationship with others' (Bradford, Gibb and Benne, 1964). This purpose is realised as people learn how to give help to others in their learning process, i.e. to make available perceptions and feelings about group members and events in the form of feedback.

Yet, as Bion (1961) noticed, there are many ways in which the group process may be blocked or diverted into the 'basic assumptions' of *dependency* (on others, especially the leaders, to do the work for one), *pairing* (interdependency or forming cliques) and *fight or flight* (ways of avoiding what is happening in the group in the present moment). Other unhelpful behaviours include scapegoating, group incongruence or deceit (Bebout, 1974), domination of the group by a few articulate individuals and attempts at hiding (e.g. if I keep very still and silent no one will notice me) by others. Many writers on groups (e.g. Bradford, Gibb and Benne, 1964; Benson, 1987; Beck, 1974) have outlined stages or phases in the group process. This tells us that what goes on in a group at the beginning of its life will be different in quality from what goes on near the end, but no theory can predict exactly what will happen in an actual group.

Key Point

Your individual style is a significant influence on how you learn. Yet much learning takes place in the context of a learning community: emotional and other factors related to being part of a group have to be taken into account.

4

Skills and Techniques

In this chapter, we consider what is meant by counselling skills and by technique in counselling. In counselling and in counselling training there remains a tension between an emphasis on the attitudes and qualities of the counsellor and on the skills and techniques involved in the practice of counselling. To some extent, this tension is addressed in the following passage:

> In our experience the counselor who tries to use a 'method' is doomed to be unsuccessful unless this method is genuinely in line with his own attitudes. On the other hand, the counselor whose attitudes are of the type which facilitate therapy may be only partially successful, because his attitudes are inadequately implemented by appropriate methods and techniques. (Rogers, 1951: 19–20)

Jenkins (1995) describes the tension as that between the deductive and the inductive models of counsellor training. His 'deductive' model is associated with 'more emphasis on the *skills* acquired and demonstrated by the practitioner, focusing on technique and proficiency' (original italics). The 'inductive' model, on the other hand, 'values experiential learning, with an emphasis on exploring *meaning*'. Jenkins's 'bottom line' – what he calls the 'shadow side' of the two models of training – is, from the deductive model, that of ending up with a 'skilled technician', suggestive of the characteristics of a robot or a computer programme; and from the inductive model, 'trainee benefit versus client benefit', the scenario in which the trainee indulges in lots of 'personal development' but doesn't know (or is less interested in) what to do to actually help the client.

It is not fruitful, in our view, merely to take sides in a debate between the merits of the inductive and the deductive models or between the qualities of the person and what they do in the counselling situation. Rather, each counsellor-in-training must engage in a dialogue in a way that can give rise to a creative integration of all of the aspects of counsellor effectiveness within their own practice.

Perhaps we might start off the dialogue in this way: How can 'skilled technicians' become counsellors with integrity, able to help others (clients) using the whole of themselves in the counselling relationship? Perhaps by clarifying their purpose and what they can offer in counselling and helping, which means having a foundation of integrated theory and values upon which to stand whilst 'applying' the skills and techniques in which they are competent.

How can an aware, 'developed' person bring to bear on the client's issues and problems a proper professional skill and appropriate technique? Perhaps by being prepared to get down to the hard, perhaps boring work of practising units of behaviour – skills – within a conscious therapeutic technique, and to receive and give feedback on the performance and efficacy of the skills in question. An analogy might be the musical 'masterclasses' that are sometimes televised in which a competent player receives detailed feedback from a 'master' not only on playing technique but also on nuances of expression and emotion.

What is meant by 'skills'?

One definition of 'skill' is 'practical ability and dexterity' (*Collins English Dictionary*, 1972). Whilst this is minimal it at least indicates that a skill is something that is *done*; it involves a behaviour which is observable and which can be learned or copied by others. In ordinary language, if someone is described as 'skilled' we understand that the person can do something and do it well.

The purpose of the word 'skill' seems to be to distinguish the part of the learning task that is not 'theory'. Perhaps the increased use of the term reflects the emphasis on practical learning away from the more theoretical view of learning that pertained in the past. It might be interesting, for example, to review the content of counsellor training courses from their inception in Britain in the 1960s until now (the late 1990s). We suspect that one of the findings might be that skills practice has taken an increasingly important place in the training curriculum. Within this emphasis on skills, we find examples of training groups such as the following, listed by Nelson-Jones (1991). It is tempting to consider that the word 'skills' could be left out without substantially altering the meaning. Here are three examples:

- Dorothy, 21, attends a course in human relations [skills] as part of her teacher training.
- Julie, 17, has some classroom periods at her secondary school in which the curriculum covers career decision-making [skills].
- Khalid, 9, participates in a class at his primary school to develop children's friendship [skills].

(Nelson-Jones, 1991: 5; square brackets added)

Skills for counselling

It is not the purpose of this book to give a comprehensive account of the whole range of skills incorporated in all counselling approaches. There are now a number of books and book chapters which describe the skills and competencies associated with counselling generically (for example, McLeod, 1993; Inskipp, 1996; Wheeler, 1996). Other written works refer to skills incorporated in specific theoretical models (Dryden, 1984; the SAGE *Counselling in Action* series; the SAGE *Counselling in Practice* series). However, many (if not most) of those undertaking counselling training are already using the basic skills and should be able to name and reflect on them. Check this out with the box below.

Develop a skill check list

What do *you* think are the essential skills that an effective counsellor should be able to demonstrate?
Which of these skills can you perform effectively?
Under which circumstances might your performance of certain skills be impaired?
What skills do you need to develop?

Learning skills for counselling

Learning a skill is distinct from learning a body of knowledge, such as counselling theory. It is learning that comes from *doing* and practising in all the senses of the word. It is the kind of learning that occurs, for example, when the learner is apprenticed to a master. Note that 'the master', in this context, can also be female (like 'actor'). Consider the following in relation to counselling:

> In a skill . . . learning is defined primarily by the exigencies of the environment and the nature of the task, rather than by any consensus interpretation of the world by society. The end product is easily recognised by the master and relatively easily by the apprentice: the well-baked loaf, the properly built wall, or whatever. Here one learns from one's mistakes . . . and these lead to modifications of perform-ance. In turn, the modifications are compiled into more effective procedures for carrying out the task. The master offers perceptions about mistakes and advice about procedures. (Oatley, 1980: 86)

Much skills training in counselling is carried out by presenting a 'product' (for example, a video or audio-tape of a counselling session) to a group of apprentices and a master (trainees and tutor) who will, together, appreciate both the good work and the 'mistakes' so that the performer knows what needs to be modified in future.

It is necessary, of course, to have seen a demonstration of the skill and to understand the significance of the skill in relation to counselling. For example, do you understand why listening is such a key skill? It has been said that listening has the same importance in counselling as watching the road has in driving a car, yet there are now 'counselling' systems without ears, in the shape of elec-tronic networks (Lago, 1996). Does a computer *listen*? Or what is its equivalent?

Competence

The idea of 'competence' is useful in conceptualising learning and in avoiding the potential reduction of behaviour into ultimately meaningless units. McLeod (1993: 94) sees competence as including both the skills and qualities 'exhibited by a competent performer in a specific occupation'. Connected with this view is the idea of four stages in learning (Clarkson and Gilbert, 1991), namely:

unconscious incompetence
conscious incompetence
conscious competence
unconscious competence

'Unconscious' is not used in a psychodynamic sense, but as 'unaware' or 'not knowing'. Consider the process of learning to drive: until you first take driving lessons, you are unaware of all the skills that you don't possess – changing gear, signalling, steering, controlling speed and so on. You soon become aware of your incompetence (and may feel pretty depressed about it!). However, by practice, you consciously and carefully perform the skills outlined above – you can observe this stage by following a learner driver nearly ready to take the driving test. Later, as an experienced driver, many of the actions (skills) are carried out without consciously thinking about them.

Moving from 'conscious incompetence' to 'conscious competence' will involve some form of 'observational learning' or 'showing people what to do' (Nelson-Jones 1991: Chapter 8). Being shown what to do can take place in a formal learning situation such as a driving lesson or in counselling training when a demonstration is given of, for example, empathic responding skills. Or it can be informal, as in a child imitating a parent to learn 'clearing-away-toys skills' or a participant in a group learning from a fellow participant how to give feedback.

Furthermore, as Nelson-Jones puts it (1991: 180), 'group leaders cannot *not* demonstrate behaviour' (italics in original); if you remain alert and observant you can learn from the way in which course tutors interact with students and others both formally and informally. (A Zen story goes that a student, on being asked how he learned from the master, said that he watched how she tied her shoelaces!) Do not be uncritical however, and remember that imitated behaviours, if they are to be of value, must ultimately be adapted to your own personality and style.

Learning a Skill

- Understand the skill and its purpose
- Watch a demonstration or read a description
- Break down the task into its discrete parts
- Try it out
- Review: How did you get on?
  - What did you feel went well?
  - Were there any problems?
  - What other factors might be impeding your performance?
    (e.g. personality/unconscious/unrealistic expectations, etc.)
  - What would have helped you to be more successful?
  - What might you do differently next time?

Examples of skills

What are some of the skills that can be learned in the ways described above? They would include:

- listening skills: e.g. attending, observing, keeping quiet
- responding skills: e.g. timing, empathic responding, paraphrasing, communicating understanding, summarising factual and emotional content
- intervention skills: e.g. challenging, confronting; questioning (open and closed); disputing; making suggestions; making interpretations

Some counselling models, notably the Skilled Helper model (Egan, 1993), see different skills as being appropriate for the different stages in the counselling process. Here is a list of the skills areas in relation to 'communication and interpersonal skills' for a three-stage model:

Stage 1:   Helping the client explore his or her concerns
           Negotiating
           Focusing/moving forward
Stage 2:   Deepening understanding
           Moving on
Stage 3:   Moving into action

                    (Adapted from Inskipp, 1996: 26,
                 where the full list of skills can be found.)

What constitutes a technique?

The term 'technique' is used in at least two ways. Firstly, it can refer to the result of a number of skills together: for example, the technique of a dancer or an artist or of a skilled therapist. And secondly (but not unconnected), technique can be used to refer to approach-specific clusters of skills, such as the two-chair technique, or 'free associative techniques' (Lambert, 1984). The 'major therapeutic techniques' of rational-emotive therapy (now known as rational emotive behaviour therapy or REBT) are listed as:

Assessment of client problems
Cognitive change techniques

Emotive-evocative change techniques
Behaviour change techniques
(Dryden, 1984: 250–1)

Each of these techniques is described in terms of distinct skills, that is, what the counsellor can (and perhaps should) *do*.

This returns us, of course, to the tension referred to above, since some approaches to counselling are resistant to describing their approach in terms of *techniques* at all, but may be willing to address the question: How do I apply the approach in practice? Thus, despite asserting that 'the existential approach does not favour technique', van Deurzen-Smith (1984: 167–70) is willing to list the following as major therapeutic techniques:

Encounter
Exploration of the subjective world-view
Enquiry into meaning
Strengthening the inner self
Establishing priorities
Making a commitment
Living

In her clarification of the technique of 'living' she writes: 'The technique is now one of reminding oneself and the client that problems are never solved and that life will always remain full of obstacles and crises' (van Deurzen-Smith, 1984: 170).

This, of course, brings us back to the question of the counsellor's beliefs, values and attitudes and how these must align with, and in some sense define, the techniques that the counsellor-in-trainig must learn and use.

Skills must be contextualised in practice

Skills may be learned as discrete units (see, for example, Inskipp, 1996) but the use of skills must be embedded in a context of practice which is systematic and underpinned by a coherent theoretical foundation. For example, the following list of skills comes from a counselling approach known as the 'perceptual process model' (Toukmanian, 1996: 207):

Use of open-ended questions
Focused probes

Reflections of perceived affect
Use of metaphoric language
Engaging clients in an in-depth exploration of perceived meanings
    and meaning associations

Learning and developing these skills, therefore, has to be in the context of segments of actual counselling sessions, perhaps in a supervision group conducted as part of the course, or in individual supervision itself.

Metaskills

There are certain skills or abilities that function at a different level from the skills mentioned earlier. By this we mean that they affect the learning and performing of these skills at a meta-level and have implications for learning and writing about skill development. We refer in particular to the skills of *thinking* and *will*.

Thinking

We may not consider the act of 'thinking' to be a distinct skill, in the sense that it can be learned and consciously practised (Nelson-Jones, 1996a). Thinking is an unseen skill or 'covert behaviour' (Nelson-Jones, 1991: 198) along with its close relation, 'self-talk'. We have the capacity to *think* about *thinking*. You might start by asking yourself:

How do I think?
What do I think?
What do I mean?

As well as thinking about your own thought processes, it is important to cultivate the habit of questioning the thinking of others. This is the basis of *critical* or *analytical* thinking. Both the merits and the flaws in others' thinking will be represented in their written work. Just because something is in print and even published does not mean that it is correct, either in content or in presentation (structure and language). Become discriminating and develop your own judgement as to what is good and what is bad, or could be better.

Ways of thinking can be positive and helpful or negative and damaging. Cognitive approaches in counselling encourage us to identify, dispute and reformulate *irrational beliefs* and *unrealistic personal rules* (see, for example, Nelson-Jones, 1991: Chapter 8; Dryden, 1990). For example, in relation to course work, a cognitive error might be: 'I won't be able to understand theory, because I got low marks at school.' Disputing this belief includes asking, 'Were my school marks really so bad?' and, 'Even if my school marks were bad, this is different because I want to learn and I can also see the theory in action.' Students often cling to the belief that 'I shouldn't have to write essays on theory because this has nothing to do with being a good counsellor.' Such a view is often associated with the 'as long as I have the right attitude, I can help' school of counselling – to dispute this, see the quotation from Carl Rogers at the beginning of this chapter.

An unrealistic personal rule might be: 'I can't ask for help from course tutors. I should do it all myself.' Of course, you cannot expect tutors to do the work for you, but is that the same as asking for specific help? And how do you feel about other people asking for help?

Another skill or technique, applicable both in counselling and in studying, is that of *coping self-talk*. There are two parts to this: calming self-talk and coaching self-talk (Nelson-Jones, 1991: 190). The first contains phrases like 'stay calm' and 'you can cope'; the second is used to specify goals, break tasks down into manageable units and to concentrate on the task at hand. Thus, if you are feeling overwhelmed by a piece of work that you have to do, you might start by sitting still, paying attention to your breathing while saying to yourself, 'Stay calm, don't get anxious, you'll get this done.'

Then you can think about and list each of the tasks involved: reading and research, the main ideas to be discussed, make a draft outline, check out a certain article and so on. Set goals: tonight, I will read that chapter and make notes on 'self-talk'; or, I will write freely for fifteen minutes and see what comes up; or, today, I will revise Chapter 4. Having specific goals is usually better than simply forcing yourself to stay at work for a certain time, say, until ten o'clock. It can be a good idea, nevertheless, to be clear before you begin, to decide on a realistic ending time. Keep to the time decided, or make a conscious redecision to work a little longer. Don't just override your own decision; if you do, you are liable to lose trust in yourself.

It is perhaps surprising to realise that cognitive approaches in counselling and spiritual disciplines such as Zen and Sufism have similar views that *thoughts* or *thought forms* are generated in the mind, propagated and continue to influence the person's life in many ways, rather like the reverberation of an echo. These approaches also agree that we can become conscious of forming our thoughts and can, with discipline, review and restructure our thinking. As Pir Vilayat Inayat Khan (1982) says: 'Our everyday sense of ourselves circumscribes us within a frontier or boundary that is purely in the mind'.

The skilful will
The boundary can be extended by learning to use the 'psychological function' of *will* (Assagioli, 1990). This does not mean simply to strengthen one's will and force oneself to overcome resistances, but to develop a 'skilful will' which can stimulate and muster other psychological functions (Assagioli, 1990: 49). There are, he says, certain psychological laws, the understanding of which can enable us to train the will to act skilfully. Here are some of his ideas:

1. The basis of all visualisation techniques is that 'images or mental pictures and ideas tend to produce . . . the external acts that correspond to them'. Visualise yourself sitting at the word-processor and writing.
2. This works reciprocally since carrying out actions and adopting attitudes 'evoke and strengthen positive and desired inner states'. Having written part or all of the assignment, you now see yourself as 'a capable student', who can get work done.
3. We all know that it is easier to pay attention to something that interests us. It is less obvious that *attention tends to increase interest*. Thus, deliberately (at first) giving attention to a daunting task (like reading a heavy theoretical chapter) is likely to arouse your interest, and so you want to understand and to learn more.
4. Correspondingly, by withdrawing attention from a distracting, but interesting image, it is de-energised and its influence is reduced. It may, in fact, be necessary to substitute another image for the distracting one. For example, if you are distracted (and, in part, attracted) by depressing images of all the work you have to do, and of yourself struggling, substitute an image of your choice, perhaps of yourself with the work

finished, or of the reward you will give yourself for finishing the chapter.

5. 'Acting as if' is a familiar yet powerful technique. Singing or whistling to yourself to lend courage while walking through a dark place alone, or putting on a front of confidence going in to the boss's office to ask for an increase in salary are examples of this. Assagioli writes that Machiavelli used to put on 'gala dress' when about to write. This might be a bit strong for most of us, but it could help to change out of the old jeans and T-shirt and put on special writing clothes, and see what happens. A related idea is the tradition at some universities for students to dress up to take their final examinations.

Key Point

Although a 'skill' is difficult to define, it can be learned by observing, doing, reviewing and doing again. Counselling approach-related techniques are the context for the practice of skills. 'Higher-order' skills such as thinking and will can also be learned and developed.

---

5 *Experiential Learning*

How do I know things? How do I learn things? These are two key questions in the struggle to understand ourselves and our relation to the world. In the western world, at any rate, the most commonly held view of 'knowing' is that it is derived from conceptual thinking, and that thinking is at the heart of our being. 'Cogito ergo sum' (I think, therefore I am), the essence of Descartes' philosophy, sums up this position. The theory of experiencing (Gendlin, 1962; Bohart, 1993, 1996) could, on the other hand, be summed up as 'I experience, therefore I am.'

The primacy of experiencing

Experiencing is 'a different way of knowing than knowing through conceptual thinking' (Bohart, 1996: 199). It connects with intuition and with sensing or feeling 'patterns of meaning'. In this way, we 'know' (i.e. sense) that something is wrong in a relationship before we can think out what it is. Experiencing is a continuous process which begins at (or before) birth. Thus, the earliest learning is *experiential* (MacMillan, 1993: 133). There is some evidence that therapy is effective to the extent that it helps clients refer to their own experiencing which in turn leads to 'experiential, perceptual shifts' in the clients' processing (Bohart, 1996: 207–10). Note that 'experiencing' is not the same as referring to their 'experience', since the former has a dynamic, process quality to it.

Some research into psychotherapy supports a perceptual process model in which 'controlled exploration and in-depth analysis of . . . experiences results in the development of more differentiated and complex schematic structures that in turn mediate change in clients' perceptions leading to greater behavioral flexibility and adjustment' (Toukmanian, 1996: 201). Those who are not psychologists (or academics) may have to read this sentence several times to try to figure out what it means – an illustration, perhaps, of the difficulty in bridging the gap between researchers and practitioners. Toukmanian seems to be describing a process akin to that of experiential learning, but which is focused and guided by the therapist's interventions, whereas the experiential learning of a trainee is focused and guided by the structure of the course, by the tutors and (to some extent) by fellow students.

It would seem that all significant learning has an experiential quality. Rogers (1983) describes some of the characteristics of such learning. It involves the whole person, cognitively and affectively; it is self-initiated; it is pervasive, potentially affecting all of the learner's life; it is evaluated by the learner and '*its essence is meaning*'. This does not rule out learning from books or lectures, but implies only that the material so presented must strike some chord with the learner and contribute to his or her personal truth. This kind of learning is central not only in counsellor training but also in the counselling process itself.

How does experiential learning come about?

Another view of experiential learning is that it is 'how experience is translated into concepts which, in turn, are used as guides in the choice of new experience' (Kolb, 1984: 128). This is the basis of the Experiential Learning Model which is shown diagrammatically in Figure 5.1 as the 'learning cycle'.

Experiences vary, not only in their readiness to be 'translated into concepts', but also in the feelings and emotions which they arouse in us, the experiencers. If an experience is not 'good enough for us to bear it in awareness' (Proctor, 1991: 64) and to be available for us to reflect on it, then the learning cycle will be blocked. A good enough learning environment will therefore provide enough support to allow a wide range of experience to be borne by the learners.

Another view of learning styles

Kolb views learning ability as having four aspects: ability for concrete experience, for reflective observation, for abstract conceptualisation and for active experimentation. These abilities are aligned in two dimensions, concrete experience – abstract conceptualisation – and active experimentation – reflective observation. Different combinations of the abilities lead to Kolb's proposed four learning styles found within organisations.

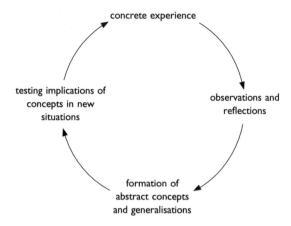

Figure 5.1   *The Experiential Learning Model* (Kolb, 1984: 128)

(a) *Converger*: abstract conceptualisation plus active experimenta-
     tion. Looks for 'the single correct answer' or solution; is rela-
     tively unemotional and inclined to prefer things to people.
     Typical occupation: engineer.
(b) *Diverger*: concrete experience plus reflective observation. Is
     imaginative, emotional, a generator of ideas, likes 'brain-
     storming'; interested in people, and liberal arts. Typical
     occupation: counsellor, personnel manager.
(c) *Assimilator*: abstract conceptualisation and reflective observa-
     tion. Creates theoretical models, reasons inductively, inclined
     towards pure science and mathematics. Typical occupation:
     researcher.
(d) *Accommodator*: concrete experience and active experimenta-
     tion. Prefers 'doing things'; adapts to circumstances; a risk-
     taker who is ready to discard theory in favour of trial-and-
     error approach; 'pushy'. Typical occupation: sales and
     marketing.

Few people (if any) would have a 'pure' learning style, yet most
are likely to incline towards one of those mentioned. Although
only one (diverger) is said to be found, typically, in counselling –
perhaps in one of the humanistic approaches? – it is interesting to
speculate what approaches to counselling might attract the others.
Would a 'converger' be drawn to solution-focused therapy? Could

the REBT counsellor be seen as a salesperson (effective in persuading clients to 'buy' what they need) and so on?

Features of experiential learning

Combs (1989: 80) lists seven principles of experiential learning. It is, he writes:

1 Essentially a process of discovering personal meaning
2 A deeply personal experience
3 Motivated by the organism's basic need
4 Critically affected by the learner's concept of self
5 Helped or hindered greatly by the learner's experience of challenge or threat
6 Deeply influenced by the learner's experience of identification or belonging
7 Critically influenced by feedback or knowledge of results.

How do these principles translate into what may happen on a training course? How is experiencing distilled into learning and personal meaning? Let us look at some possibilities.

Implicit theories
The notion of 'implicit theories' can help us understand the nature of personal meaning – and, thus, the nature of personal learning. Oatley (1980: 91), following Karen Horney, suggests that 'everyone evolves some implicit theories based on innate predispositions and on their interactions with significant others in their early lives'. Personal learning is thus 'the extension or modification of an implicit theory' which is the basis of personal meaning.

If the core theoretical model of the training course is to carry personal meaning for us, we have to be able to integrate it with our implicit theory, our beliefs and values. How does the core model of counselling fit your experience and beliefs about yourself and other people? In what ways does it not fit? At the beginning of training (and as a counsellor starting out) a need for security can make one hang on to the theory so much that everything is made to fit it, including clients and oneself. Attending to one's direct experience of how people really are can be uncomfortable, if the experience and the theory do not fit together. This 'lack of fit' is known as *dissonance*.

Dissonance
The concept of dissonance is useful in explaining how we learn from experience. Dissonance is set up by experiencing which is inconsistent with a belief or attitude or which does not fit the implicit theory. Mearns (1995: 89–91) sees dissonance as playing a key part in relation to self-concept change, which is a specific instance of learning, or re-learning, who you are. Dissonance sets up a tension within the belief system, which is reduced either by denying the new experience or by incorporating it into the existing belief system and thereby changing one's perception of the experience. This, in effect, is what is meant by 'learning' or 'acquiring knowledge'. If the tension is too much to bear, that is if the situation is so challenging as to be threatening, denial and reversion to the status quo is the most likely outcome.

For example, if my value system is such that showing annoyance is unacceptable behaviour, I may believe that I am someone who does not get annoyed. However, should I be confronted in an experiential group with evidence of my behaving like an annoyed person, either I will have to change my perception of myself or continue to deny my own experiencing and feeling of annoyance. If I can allow my perception of myself to change (and this is more likely to happen in a supportive environment) I have learned something significant. Without the stimulus of new experiencing, no learning will occur. The optimum condition for learning is thus provided by challenge plus support.

Concept of self
Students on a training course may have a wide variety of experience in counselling. On a diploma course, for instance, some students may only have experience of practising counselling skills, say, in their workplace. Others may practise counselling with a voluntary agency and yet others may be employed as counsellors, in an educational institution for example. It has been possible, in the past, to be appointed to a counselling post without having acquired a counselling qualification that would now be considered necessary for such a job.

How does this mix affect the students on the course? Probably, some of the less experienced trainees will feel inadequate beside those who are counselling every day, whilst the experienced practitioners may well feel put on the spot and expected to perform by the book. Some of the latter may indeed believe that they know all about it (counselling practice, that is) and so will be unable to learn until they can set this attitude aside. Others may never have had to expose their practice to anyone other than a supervisor and may be very anxious that all their faults will be shown up in front of others as well as themselves. Many course members may therefore compare themselves unfavourably with their fellow students and be anxious about exposing their 'failings' to others in the belief that this would be an uncomfortable experience.

Challenge or threat
The line between what is experienced as 'challenging' and what is experienced as 'threatening' may be very finely drawn. An aspect of training which can challenge or threaten counselling trainees is that of feeling, or indeed becoming, de-skilled as the course progresses. Analogous to learning to drive, when the learner finds it necessary to become conscious of and eradicate bad habits that may have built up before the course of instruction was undertaken, counselling trainees (especially those with previous experience in a counselling role) can find that the course challenges behaviour that they thought was skilful. This can create a threatening dissonance, especially if the trainee has to turn up for work as a counsellor every day. At the same time, their less experienced colleagues may feel threatened by those whom they consider to more proficient than they are. This is a challenge to both groups, those 'with experience' and those without.

If the challenge becomes a threat (to self-esteem, for example) the learning process may be blocked. The block can be tackled either at the feeling level or the behaviour level, or both. That means that the trainee counsellor's anxiety needs to be expressed and acknowledged, helping to ease them into the behaviour, and the behaviour (e.g. engaging in skills practice) carried out despite the anxiety. Both of these steps will be easier if some trust has developed within the group of students and tutors. Feedback, given appropriately, helps to build trust and to help people see themselves more clearly as they gain information about how others see them.

Identification and belonging
How trainee counsellors perceive themselves affects their sense of identification with the training group and their sense of belonging to it. There are many reasons why people feel they do not belong

to a group. Perhaps they have had experiences of being judged negatively, or have been rejected in the past and treated as an outsider. Such experiences are all too common in everyday life. On a training course, there are several groups with which trainees can identify. There is the whole learning cohort itself, the 'class of 96' or whenever. There will be various sub-groups, such as personal learning groups or the equivalent, study groups, a group of trainees who travel on the same train, and so on. Another sense of belonging can arise from identification with the core theoretical model of the course, the counselling world view, as it were. Belongingness and identification will fluctuate in intensity. Yet, sometimes a trainee may feel quite overwhelmed by the course and all it may imply about conformity to the model and identification with the counselling world view – the 'initiatory element' (Purton, 1991: 47). This may in fact be a normal and healthy stage in the development of one's personal stance and style in counselling.

Feedback

There is an art in giving and receiving feedback. Combs (1989: 91) reminds us that feedback is most likely to be effective when it is immediate and continuous, personal, challenging and relevant. Some of the contexts for feedback in counselling training are skills practice sessions, interactive group sessions and individual feedback from tutors relating to written assignments and counselling practice. The first two are perhaps the most significant as far as experiential learning is concerned.

Supervision is also an occasion for feedback, but supervisors may be separate from the course team. If, as a student, you do not feel you are getting enough feedback, or if the feedback is primarily judgemental and critical, consider asking for a meeting with the course tutors to discuss how feedback could be given in a more helpful way. If the college has a system of student representatives or staff–student councils, negotiation can be carried out through them.

When you are at the receiving end of feedback, try to be open to whatever helpful information may be in it for you, rather than to defend yourself against it. Remember that you do not have to agree with another person's opinion. It is most useful if a number of people give feedback to give a fuller picture.

When giving feedback, the rule is to be honest and own your opinion as your own. Refer to concrete aspects of behaviour whenever possible, state your genuine reaction and offer alternative suggestions tentatively rather than dogmatically. This is useful practice for the feedback you may give to clients in a counselling relationship.

Key Point

Experiencing holds a primary place in the process of learning. Experiential learning is a continuous process of experiencing, reflecting and becoming open to new experience. Its essence is personal meaning. This learning is inhibited by threat and enhanced by challenging and supportive feedback.

Part II

Communicating Learning

6

How Do I Know What I Mean Unless I Say (Or Write) It?

In Part II, we consider the communication of what has been learned and the special place of writing in this process. Learning and communicating, as we have seen in Chapter 5, are closely linked. Learning feeds into communicating and by communicating, our learning can be taken even further. This is not only a verbal process. For example, in the case of a piece of music, the composer's learned skills and knowledge take form in the composition, the musician's learning is communicated in the playing and the audience hear and are changed by the performance, which they listen to through the filter of their own previous learning. The composer and musicians will also learn through composing and playing, which are part of the communication of their learning.

Communication on a counsellor training course takes place in a number of contexts. These include:

discussion – formal and informal
tutorials and consultation with tutors
conversations with fellow students
personal development groups
feedback – giving and receiving
personal writing (notes, letters, journals)
written assignments

Communication, in all of these contexts, may be said to have two functions. First, it is a way of *demonstrating*, or a guide to, what has been learned, and second, it is itself a *means* or a vehicle for further learning to take place. There is therefore both a static and a dynamic element in communication.

The 'static' aspect of communication

Written communication is more generally associated with the static element – it stays, after all, on the page as it has been written – and spoken communication with the dynamic element. Part of one's reluctance to start writing can be because of the apparent fixedness of what is written down. There it stands, in black and white, and is the grounds on which judgement or assessment is made, even if, immediately after the assignment is submitted, the views of the writer develop and change. The assignment is a snapshot taken in the process of learning. The box below tells how one of the authors described her feelings about writing an essay.

Prologue to a written assignment

I don't want to write this essay because it means I will have to *fix* things somehow – in words, in print, in time – while I'm really in *flux*. I'm in the middle of a process and the theme of this essay [power] reflects some of that process: it reflects what is going on for me, what is engaging me *now*, and my concerns will move on, I know. At the same time, part of me is pleased to be writing this because I'll be able to look back on it from wherever I am in the future and catch a glimpse of where I am now.

A piece of writing may be like a 'snapshot', and may or may not present a 'good picture' of its subject, yet it can also be like a 'product' or an end-point in a process. Sometimes, as a combination of sufficient preparation, interest and enthusiasm in the subject and ease of using language, an essay almost seems to write itself. Even if this ease is not achieved (and it is rare, in our experience) it may be clear that the thing just has to get written so that you, the author, can move on to the next stage. The knack is to know when the time for this has come and to resist continuing to 'prepare' (thinking, reading and planning) and thus going past the point when it needs to be got out of your system.

The dynamic element of communication

'How do I know what I mean unless I talk about it?' might almost be a motto for counselling itself. It is by talking aloud, saying it out to another person that the contents of one's mind can be made manifest and looked at to find the meaning that resides within. It has been said that education is a forum for the negotiation of meaning (Bruner, 1986). By talking with others (including counsellors), reading what others have written and by our own writing (journal, assignments, letters, papers, books) we are negotiating the meaning of our experience for ourselves. We may also add to the process of negotiating meaning for others.

A further stage is added to the path of learning that leads through hearing or reading about something (for example, a counselling skill such as 'challenging'), witnessing this being carried out by someone else (watching a demonstration interview) then doing it oneself (practising 'challenging' in a skills session or as a counsellor oneself). Writing can help to distil the experience through all of the stages, as well as describe that experience to others. The box below is an extract from a written assignment which describes how the dynamic aspect of writing takes learning forward.

Conclusion to an assignment

I've got to stop writing now. I'm aware that this assignment will be on the long side, but I've thoroughly enjoyed writing it, all on one day. The writing itself felt like a mini process echoing the longer one that started in early January (and the even longer one that started in 1989, and the one beyond that . . .!). The content goes from my past, through my experiences and reading, ending up at the insights I've had on person-centred and Gestalt therapy in just the last twenty-four hours. (Writing this hasn't been just such a 'tiny part' of the process as anticipated at the start.) And I'm excited by what I've learnt.

I feel that the areas discussed at the end – style, power, modes of expression – are all ones that I can continue to learn in. Indeed the contribution of writing this is to produce a clearer focus for my own learning. So I'm back at my continuum again, from my personal experience to an external body of knowledge, which itself consists of human experience and is made up of a complex mixture of ideas and the personalities of those who developed them.

It fits with the dynamism of writing that you do not have to know everything or know it perfectly before you start to write. Books and articles in print can seem established and concrete compared to the personal learning process which keeps changing and includes areas which are not known. The prospect of integrating theory and experience in writing is particularly challenging in the field of counselling because of the personal nature of much of the learning. It can be freeing when you begin to write, simply to state what you do not know. Thus wrote Carl Rogers:

> I find that another way of learning for me is to state my own uncertainties, to try to clarify my puzzlements, and thus get closer to the meaning that my experience actually seems to have. (Kirschenbaum and Henderson, 1990: 303)

The conclusion to a piece of work can also, quite appropriately, state areas of not-knowing and indicate where further research is needed, whether it is undertaken individually or in the academic community.

Choosing the right word

'Say what you have to say as simply and directly as possible in order that you may be readily understood' (Gowers, 1973: 98) is probably the best single rule for effective writing. However, prescribing simplicity and directness does not imply that a limited vocabulary is all that is needed, it merely counsels against pretentious and convoluted writing. A wide and precise vocabulary is an essential aid to the articulation of the subtleties of feeling as well as to the accurate representation of the understanding of theory.

Perhaps the best way of expanding your vocabulary is by widening your reading. Do not stop at reading material which you already like and understand. Try out unfamiliar and perhaps initially difficult texts, and note the words whose meaning is new to you. You may also note words that you particularly like or that you find especially expressive. Become familiar (if you are not already) with books in the body of literature and with poetry, at least in order to give you some ideas about how language can be used. Nor should the fields of science and technology be neglected. It is also educational to explore the writings of a culture other than your own, which may be closer to the cultural background of your clients. Not only writing, but also plays, films and video material can be used to add to your vocabulary and means of expression.

Creative modes of expression

Lively and imaginative writing is a pleasure to read as well as satisfying to write. It is likely to include the use of metaphor and similar expressive modes of language. The most effective metaphor is one which has personal meaning for the writer. It is less effective and will appear artificial to take over a metaphor from someone else. Toukmanian (1996: 200) has pointed out that the 'facilitative power' of metaphoric language in therapy depends on both therapist and client understanding and elaborating the metaphor. Similarly, the effective use of metaphor in writing depends on both writer and reader associating some personal meaning with it. The reader, in the case of academic assignments, may be the tutor who is going to assess your work. Avoid, therefore, metaphors which can have meaning only for you or a very limited group of people. You may, of course, explain the metaphor as in this example from Mearns and Thorne (1988: 49 and 58): 'It feels like being a Celtic supporter at the Rangers end' is explained by the footnote, 'Being a "Celtic supporter at the Rangers end" would represent extreme social isolation tinged with an element of danger!' This metaphor can be seen to be culturally and a touch gender specific.

The importance of questions

Rogers, in the sentence quoted on p. 60, seems to be saying, 'How do I know what I mean unless I state what I don't know and what my questions are?' It is important, in the search for knowledge for each of us to clarify what our own questions are. Defining what we don't know and what we are looking for brings a focus to our reading, where the SQ3R approach (Rowntree, 1970) tells us never to read without having some questions in mind. SQ3R is Survey, Question, Read, Recall, Review.

Just as counselling has been described as 'personal research' (O'Hara, 1986; MacMillan, 1993), so we can understand learning on a counselling training course as 'personal research' in a slightly different sense. The difference is that, rather than the research effort being concentrated between two people (client and counsellor) it is diffused throughout the whole context of the training course. Nevertheless, certain principles remain valid: the need for a question or questions to focus and drive the research and the view of writing as resembling 'research reports', which both give a picture of the current (static) situation and of the process of search with its failures (apparently), successes and unknown areas still to be explored.

The experiences derived from writers' workshops have a similar flavour (Kirkwood, 1990). In the early 1980s the Workers Educational Association fostered a number of writers' workshops in Edinburgh the values of which have some relevance to undertaking training in counselling, especially when the trainee has been away from formal education for some time, or has had a negative experience of it in the first place.

> First, the writers' workshop movement tends to encourage the involvement of anyone, not just those likely to succeed; those who left school at the earliest opportunity, who did badly at school or did not enjoy school; those who have experienced, as adults, work situations which do not give outlets for their creativity or sense of responsibility . . . Second, it places great emphasis on writing about personal experiences: writing is seen as a means of exploring, expressing, recreating, celebrating and reflecting upon actual experiences the writer has had, good or bad. (Kirkwood, 1990: 267)

The difference in counselling training, of course, is that it is not only about personal experience; it must also include that body of theoretical knowledge that can be accessed in the writings of the 'elders' in the counselling field.

Assignments – the challenge

Even when seen in the light of being an integral part of learning, the prospect of writing set pieces of work can still feel daunting and raises several issues.

- The evaluation component in assignments may raise feelings of being judged or criticised. Maybe you have been found 'not good enough' in the past; or you have excelled in the past. These experiences may colour your approach to assignments now.
- You may feel that your skills are rusty. The chapters which follow in Part II look at some of the skills needed for effective academic work and study, such as reading, note-taking, writing, structuring your work, using language correctly.

■ The prospect of analysing your work with a client may be a new and different challenge. It will involve finding a balance between theoretical reflection and a review of your personal skills. Your own investment in the work you have done with a client may be considerable and writing about it may feel like laying yourself on the line. Chapter 13 looks specifically at writing about practice.

Key Point

Writing can be both an end in itself by communicating what you have learned (e.g. in written assignments) and a means to develop your learning on the course. Expanding your vocabulary and developing imaginative ways of expression lead to greater depths of meaning in both static and dynamic aspects of writing. Generating your own questions helps focus both the learning and the writing.

7

The Requirements of the Course: Assessment

It is likely that you will be investing a considerable amount of time, money and energy in the training course. Understandably, you would like it to be an enjoyable, interesting and enriching experience. You would also like to learn about counselling and the practice of counselling or counselling skills, perhaps to the standard of being prepared for starting out as a professional counsellor.

However, you will also have to meet the standards and fulfil the assessment criteria set by the course. The course brochure or prospectus should include basic information about the following:

- the assessment procedure
- required written work
- the assessment schedule
- how practice is assessed
- which is the accrediting body
- what qualification is awarded at the end of the course
- what happens if a trainee does not complete the course or fails (is there any outcome/intermediate or 'step-off' award?)
- the appeals procedure

It is likely that specific assessment guidelines will not be given at this stage, but they should be outlined in the course handbook.

When you are reading the information given, bear in mind these questions:

What do I have to do on this course?
When do I have to do it?

What (if any) choice do I have?
How much is needed to pass?

Assessment and assessment criteria

Assessment criteria cover two aspects:

1   Overall (aggregate) criteria for passing the course
2   Specific criteria for passing each assignment.

Completing, or passing, all assignments would be one of the aggregate criteria, but is not usually enough in itself. Other requirements include adequate attendance on the course, completion of placement hours, satisfactory supervision reports, submission of audio-tapes of counselling work and satisfying the rules of ethical practice, plus evidence of appropriate self-awareness and personality factors suitable for counselling.

There will almost certainly be a time limit for completion of all course components. Courses, especially post-graduate, within an academic institution will come under the overarching regulations for submission (and resubmission) and completion of assignments. There should be an appeals procedure for use in the event of a dispute.

Do read carefully the information on assessment given in the course literature. Ask about any part of it that you do not understand. The context for assessment on professional counsellor training courses is described in Dryden, Horton and Mearns (1995: Chapter 12). You can find sample assessment criteria as an appendix to *Developing Counsellor Training* (Dryden and Feltham, 1994: 135–7).

Assessment is often the most worrying aspect of the course for a participant. Even someone who is normally confident about their abilities is likely to be nervous at the prospect of being judged and it is therefore important for it to be explained clearly what assessment will involve. This explanation may be given in the course handbook, by course tutors, in the assessment regulations of the institution or all three.

It has been pointed out (Dryden, Horton and Mearns, 1995: 133) that the role of course staff in making the definitive judgements about who passes the course and who does not, sits somewhat uneasily with the role of the same staff in giving students support

by encouraging, listening to them and understanding their difficulties. To some extent (but not entirely) the discomfort is relieved
by placing the first role within the *summative* and the second
within the *formative* assessment process. For a fuller explanation
of these terms, see below in this chapter. A clear exposition of the
difficulties inherent in assessment is given by Inskipp, who writes:

> Counselling, whatever the theory, is based on respect and acceptance
> of the client as a person, and we as trainers need to model this in our
> work with trainees. This creates difficulties when the trainer has to take
> on the role of assessor with authority and power to pass or fail.
> (Inskipp, 1996: 69)

Both trainers and trainees have to realise that trainers (course
tutors) are not in the same role as counsellors and that the tutor–
trainee relationship is not the same as the counsellor–client relationship, whatever the model of counselling. Perhaps the roles are
not so different in those models of counselling in which the
counsellor is more directive or takes on more of the functions of an
expert. Nevertheless, most courses take into consideration
elements of tutor, peer and self-assessment. (For an example of
how this is structured on an integrative course, see Inskipp, 1996:
71–2.)
    Two questions arise:

1   Which of these (tutors, peers or the trainees themselves) has
    the *final* authority to pass (or fail) the student and make the
    award of the course qualification? It is most usual to find that
    the final decision is made by the course staff. There are a few
    courses (usually training in the person-centred approach)
    which give the final authority to the students themselves. We
    do not know of any courses which give the final decision over
    to the peer group of students.
2   To what extent is the assessment of others (i.e. not those who
    have the 'final authority') taken into account in the summative
    assessment? Part of the answer to this question can be found
    in the structures or frameworks within which these assess-
    ments can be made. For example, how (and how often) is
    feedback given and how is it recorded? Are tutors available for
    consultation by students? Is students' written work circulated
    to other students? How is written work graded and by whom?

The kind of structures and frameworks available indicate the extent to which assessment is an 'open' rather than a 'closed' or 'controlled' procedure. An open procedure is less imposing and may give more choice within it regarding the assessment tasks. Students may even be able to suggest their own title and subject for an essay (usually in consultation with course staff) and may also be involved in negotiating the assessment criteria. The amount of choice varies a great deal and is again likely to be related to the theoretical model of the course. Cognitive-behavioural, psychodynamic and other models in which a large amount of theoretical knowledge must be demonstrated may be less flexible.

Resubmission of work

Ask the course staff or read the regulations concerning resubmission of work that has been assessed as not yet meeting the pass criteria. The regulations may allow for one or two resubmissions, and will also indicate the time limit within which this should be done. Many tutors are willing to pre-read essays and give informal guidance on them. It is important to be clear that such a 'trial submission' is a draft for the purpose of getting feedback and that it does not count as a final submission. One counselling skills course encourages students to submit one audio tape for practice and to receive formative feedback, before submission of a second tape for assessment.

The feedback you are given (formative evaluation) should make it clear to you what needs to be done, in addition to or instead of, what you have already submitted. For example, a student who failed to meet the performance criteria for passing an assignment requiring an audio recording of a counselling interview along with a critique of a ten-minute segment, was asked to resubmit a tape demonstrating basic empathic responding plus a summary of a chapter on congruence to show her theoretical understanding of this concept.

Formative and summative assessment

It is important to understand the difference between formative and summative assessment. *Summative* assessment is that which sums up a student's achievement (either on the whole course or on specific units of it, such as a module) and is the decision on which the final award is made – the bottom line being to pass or to fail the course.

Before that stage is reached, however, the work of the student (written assignments, skills practice and so on) will have been assessed a number of times and in a number of ways by tutors, peers and the students themselves. Feedback given in these instances is intended to help the student modify, shape and improve on what has already been done. The feedback may be informal and unstructured in such contexts as an open learning (or personal development) group, skills practice sessions, study groups and tutorials or consultations with course staff.

Feedback given to a written assignment will probably be more formal. In most cases, this would be in written form, perhaps on the assignment itself. However, at least one diploma course gives tutor feedback to written assignments on an audio-tape cassette. This provides very immediate, lively feedback, which can comfortably lead into a continuing discussion of the assignment content. It also makes the feedback less of a pronouncement 'from on high'. All of this would be part of the *formative* assessment process. Clearly, it is sensible to keep a copy of each assignment that you hand in, in case it should get lost, for example.

Depending on the course structure, there may be certain assessment points that act as 'gates' through which a student must pass before proceeding to the next part. For example, a modular certificate course may require students to pass each module, in the set order, before going on to the next. Others are structured in such a way that, although there may be assessment tasks at various stages, students are not held up even if they have to resubmit an assignment. Documentation should make it clear which of these structures is in place (or a different structure).

What is assessed and how

You should expect that all components of the course will be assessed. These are likely to be described as theory, skills, personal development and client work/practice. Let us look at how each may be assessed.

Theory

Both the understanding of theory and the application of theory will be assessed. Theoretical understanding will be broad enough to

Feedback to a written assignment for a module on 'self and group process'

This is a well-structured essay that is both easy and interesting to read. I liked the way that you described some of the theoretical ideas from the literature then looked at the group experience of the module in that light.

You combined a personal viewpoint and reporting of your own experiencing with an 'objective' stance informed by the theory. I think you have made very good use of your diary of the module. It gives this assignment a real and vivid sense.

Some of the themes you have touched on are: the need for a feeling of safety for group members to be able to speak openly, and how that safety can be compromised for quite a time by an unresolved conflict between group members; the value of feeling recognised and supported; an appreciation of the stages of the group, how the group changes with time.

This module has raised some questions for you to which you are giving serious consideration e.g. the importance of being true to your own style of group leadership; whether 'counselling' is for you (or maybe you need to find your own style in that, too). It adds up to you taking responsibility for your own learning but, in doing so, challenging others, whether tutors or colleagues, to respond to you in the same spirit.

This submission fulfils the assignment criteria and is a PASS.

include other approaches as well as the core theoretical model. 'Application' includes applying the theory to your own experience as well as to your counselling (or counselling skills) practice. Assessment is likely to be by written assignments, which will vary in length and depth of analysis according to the level of the course. At post-graduate level, analytical writing rather than simply descriptive writing will be expected. A wide knowledge of the literature will be needed to fulfil the assignment criteria. The criteria themselves will be closely linked with the learning outcomes for the relevant modules. These learning outcomes vary and become more complex at different course levels. The box on p. 71 lists learning outcomes at four different levels (up to Master's degree standard) for one university.

Skills
Assessment of skills is likely to be continuous throughout the course, in small practice groups, for example. Skills may also be assessed through the medium of audio or video-recording of

counselling sessions. The tape can be used for interpersonal process recall (IPR) (Kagan, 1984) leading to formative assessment. A
detailed description of a skills training session using IPR is given by
Inskipp (1996: 97–100). A common approach to skills assessment
involves students selecting a passage from such a tape and submitting it along with a written transcript and an analysis of their own
performance as counsellor or counselling skills user. Additional
formative feedback will be given by the counselling supervisor.

Personal development
This is perhaps the most difficult component to assess as there are
few, if any, objective measures that can be applied. Students may
have to use the feedback from peers and tutors to reflect on their
self-development during the course. Aspects of self-development
will include to what extent and in what ways the student has used
the opportunities offered on the course; the changes in the
student's self-awareness and self-concept (if this is a significant
construct for the core theoretical model); awareness of how the
course member has learned to handle anxiety and other emotional
factors; and reflection on how she or he has progressed in the role
of counsellor. Personal development includes some measure of
'personality factors'.

Client work/practice
To some extent this overlaps with assessment of skills, since the
submission of a tape plus analysis also provides evidence of the
trainee's counselling practice. Assessment in this area may also
involve a placement supervisor's report, a submission of a 'practice
log' to the course tutor and a written assignment in the form of a
case study of a counselling process from beginning through to its
end or nearly so. The practice log probably takes the form of a list
of clients (suitably anonymised), dates of first and subsequent
meetings with perhaps a phrase denoting the problem that brought
the person to seek counselling. For counselling skills users, a
similar log can be kept, with more information about the role that
each party has and the context of the meeting.

Academic language

The box on p. 71 provides a fine example of the kind of academic
language that is current in institutions of higher education as they

Learning outcomes by level

Level 1 The programme member will be able to:
(i) demonstrate a knowledge of the basic vocabulary and/or skills relating to the area of study
(ii) describe relevant professional problems in a clear and insightful way
(iii) present material clearly and accurately and according to accepted academic conventions
(iv) undertake learning tasks with some guidance
(v) apply the knowledge and/or skills he or she has developed appropriately to his/her own situation

Level 2 In addition to the requirements of level 1, the programme member will be able to:
(i) demonstrate a familiarity with the major conceptual framework relating to the area of study
(ii) analyse relevant professional problems using a given framework
(iii) present material in ways which communicate clearly to a professional audience
(iv) undertake learning tasks with a degree of independence
(v) apply the knowledge, understanding and/or skills which he or she has developed appropriately in a number of specified situations

Level 3 In addition to the requirements of level 2, the programme member will be able to:
(i) demonstrate a critical understanding of the major theories relating to the area of study
(ii) present arguments and analysis which incorporate ideas from a range of sources and draw reasoned conclusions from these
(iii) develop and implement independent strategies to enhance his or her own learning and to negotiate learning tasks with others
(iv) apply the knowledge, understanding and/or skills which he or she has developed appropriately in a variety of complex situations

Level M In addition to the requirements of level 3, the programme member will be able to:
(i) place his or her critical understanding of theory and practice within a wider context of the range of practice and current debates in the area of study
(ii) demonstrate the achievement of a personal synthesis of ideas based on study, reflection and experience
(iii) present material with some sophistication and originality
(iv) take full responsibility for his or her own learning
(v) demonstrate how the knowledge, understanding and/or skills he or she has developed can contribute to improved practice through a continuous process of critical reflection and consequent action

strive to give precise descriptions of what they are teaching and what they hope their students (i.e. 'programme members') are learning. Most (but not all) higher education institutions will describe the aims of their work in this way (we could almost say, 'to describe their products'). Not all agencies offering counsellor training courses use this academic language, but you will meet it in nearly all of those which are institutions of higher education.

Try not to be put off by this. Although, as a text, it is open to interpretation and deconstruction (see Chapter 14), we can take from it information about the different requirements which pertain for learning and for describing that learning at increasingly complex levels of an academic course.

For example, in Level 1, some key words are 'basic vocabulary', 'describe', 'present material' and 'apply appropriately'. At Level 2, the key terms have changed to 'major conceptual framework', 'analyse problems', and the range of situations in which learning can be applied has widened, whilst the amount of guidance given to the learner is reduced. By Level 3, 'critical understanding', 'arguments, analysis and reasoned conclusions' indicate the increased complexity of the thinking skills involved; learners are expected to become more independent and to negotiate their learning which is to be applied in even more complex situations. At Master's level (Level M), we find the requirements of 'critical understanding', 'personal synthesis', 'sophistication' and 'originality' (no longer a regurgitation of what has been read). Full responsibility is now expected to be taken for one's own learning and the learner should now have become a contributor of new learning for others leading to 'improved practice'.

Who assesses? Self, peer and tutor assessment

Throughout school, and probably throughout any subsequent further or higher education, the work of students is assessed by teachers and tutors. Teachers and tutors (in this scheme of things) are seen as the ones who know best and can judge the person's work objectively. If this view were carried into counsellor training, it would not foster the development of reflective practitioners at any level of counselling or counselling skills practice. A significant element of self-evaluation should, therefore, be part of the total assessment process, although how significant will depend on the theoretical model of the course. It is probably greatest for person-centred courses.

Some self-evaluation can be incorporated most easily into the assessing of skills proficiency and participation in self-development groups. Indeed, it could hardly be left out of those contexts. If group working is a large element of the training approach on the course (and it is not so for every course), individual self-evaluation becomes part of the group's evaluation of itself.

Co-operating in the assessment of one's own work and the work of others is very different from traditional educational methods. We may have memories of huddling over our desks in primary school, with a protective arm wrapped around the jotter, elbows pointed at neighbours conveying the message that they were not to look. The awarding of marks and grades for work leads also to competition and comparison amongst peers, which is hardly compatible with the recognition that, especially in counsellor training, learning cannot take place in isolation from others.

A self-assessed course?

At the beginning of this chapter, we outlined some assessment requirements for courses. Yet, perhaps the most significant variable is whether or not the course is self-assessing when it comes to the final award of the diploma in counselling. (To the best of our knowledge there are no certificate courses which are self-assessed at the summative level.) Most courses have an element of self-evaluation, whether or not it is formally incorporated into the assessment schedule, but most of these reserve to the course staff the right to award the final diploma. A few, however, are open to awarding the diploma on the basis of the student's self-appraisal, provided that all other structural requirements of the course have been completed. Thus there is a vital difference in where the ultimate power resides – in the course members themselves or in the tutors.

Do not imagine, however, that having the power to award oneself a diploma in counselling (all course requirements having been met) is the easy option. The self-assessment process involves consulting with peer course members, placement supervisor and course tutors. Thus, one must lay oneself on the line as a counsellor-in-training, open and receptive to other people's perceptions without losing touch with one's own perception of oneself. In the end, the objective is to come as close to a realistic self-perception and evaluation as is possible. Then, this must be expressed in writing in the self-evaluative statement. A student on one such course described this as 'the most telling piece of writing that I have ever undertaken'.

Deciding to award oneself a diploma in counselling is one culmination of the commitment to the training course that began (formally, at any rate) at the start of the course. In real measure, it means *owning* the award of the diploma. It may also mean owning a decision to defer the award until such time as one has gained more practical experience or clarified one's theoretical stance or completed a period of further personal counselling. Thus, the course member comes to experience what 'taking responsibility for oneself' can mean in reality.

We must emphasise that this degree of self-assessment is rarely found, and possibly only in courses training in the person-centred approach. However, in Scotland, at any rate, there are roughly sixty students each year graduating from a university course with such an assessment procedure (a high proportion of the counselling trainees in this country) and the very fact that many (probably most) other institutions of higher education would imagine such an assessment procedure to be impossible to carry out merits its mention here.

Key Point

It is essential that you ascertain the requirements of the course and details of its assessment procedures. Who assesses is a key issue, particularly the degree of self-assessment. A self-assessed course provides a particular challenge.

8

Starting to Write

Some people find it difficult to write, especially if they have not been used to doing so. There is something about writing things down that feels so *permanent*, in a way that saying the same things does not. What if I write this as my opinion now and later I realise that I have changed my mind? Writing may also feel very exposing of oneself and one's ideas to outside judgement. This is reality, in the sense that course assignments will be assessed in some way. Members of counselling training courses cannot even take refuge in turning out 'objective' academic work, for oneself and one's own experience are often the very stuff of the writing. Thus, even those people who find that writing comes easily to them may have to adjust either to writing more personally (if their previous writing experience has been largely academic) or to writing not only personally but also in a way that fulfils the academic requirements of the course.

Personal journal

Many courses either require students to keep a personal journal or strongly encourage it. In any case a journal or diary is a good way to get into (or back into) writing. Check out whether or not you will have to hand over a journal to be read by course staff. It is our opinion that this is not a good practice since it does not allow students the freedom to write without censoring themselves. It is important to have a place for writing that is just for you alone.

Such a journal can be structured in any way you please. 'Stream of consciousness' writing is a good way to capture your thoughts just as they pass through your mind. Unfortunately it does not always make much sense to you when you read it over later. Some unstructured jottings are less than helpful if you wish to use them as a basis for a self-evaluation of your learning on the course.

As one diploma student wrote:

I have never been able to keep any kind of journal or diary for long. The only things that resemble some kind of primitive note-keeping are the brief scrawls in the Filofax – 'chez E' or 'saw T', followed by small drawings that remind me of significant events. It would have been most helpful for the writing of this assignment had I adopted a different style this time. (Marylou Andriakopoulou, 1996)

Template for a daily journal

Date:

Today's sessions:

What were the significant episodes for me today?

What demands were made on me as a participant and how did I meet them?

What feelings do I recollect and what were they linked to?

What questions am I asking?

What significant things am I learning?

How does this link to my learning agenda and the demands of the course?

Observations about myself, other participants, the tutors, the content.

On recording personal learning

The following suggestions may also help you to keep record of what you are learning while on the course.

1. If you are finding it difficult to start writing at any time, it may help to begin with any images or feelings that you are experiencing at the moment.
2. It can be useful to think about what has happened during the day in terms of episodes, where an episode is a sequence of actions, with a beginning and an end, that somehow makes sense on its own. You could write about what happened

during an episode, what you felt about it, what significance it
had for other people, and so on.
3. You may wish to write about how your relationship with other
course members developed during each day and throughout
the duration of the course. Alternatively, you may do this
diagrammatically.
4. Most important of all is to write about yourself, what you are
feeling and thinking, what learning takes place for you and
what learning you may have contributed to for others.

Writing practice

The main thing is actually to start writing, however it comes out.
Natalie Goldberg, writing guru, reminds us that 'reading a book
about writing is different from actually getting down and doing
writing' (1991: xiv). Goldberg's 'rules of writing practice' can
equally be applied to writing as a student on a counselling training
course as to a student of creative writing. The foundation of
writing, she says is 'learning to trust your own mind'.

Her other rules are:

Keep your hand moving – once you begin to write, keep going
for a set time without stopping. This is so that you do not mix up
the creative and editing aspects of writing. Who hasn't worked for
a time with only a heap of crumpled pages, all attempts at starting
the same piece, to show for their efforts? If you work directly on
to the keyboard, the same principle applies. Keep keying, avoid
quick use of the delete key and print out a hard copy that you can
read over before editing.

Lose control – say what you want to say without trying to figure
out what *they* want you to say or what the 'correct form' would
be. That can be attended to later in the process of editing.

Be specific – 'Not fruit, but apple. Not bird, but wren.'
Goldberg's advice for creative writing applies to course writing
also. Not 'a lot of transference was happening in the group' but 'P
seemed to dare me to tell him off for leaving the group early. I
resisted the temptation to get cross with him, the way my mother
would have done.'

Don't think – this can really seem a perverse piece of advice in relation to academic writing, but what Goldberg is getting at is that thoughts, second thoughts and third and fourth thoughts, distract or censor the first flash of inspiration. Better to keep your hand moving and allow this first line to develop; editing (thinking) comes later.

There are three further rules:

Don't worry about punctuation, spelling, grammar – not at the beginning stage; these can all be sorted out later, with help, if necessary.

You are free to write the worst junk anywhere – again, this helps to free you up. Sometimes, students coming into a college counselling service are afraid to start an essay because they 'know it is going to be so bad'. It can be suggested that they deliberately set out to write a bad piece of work. If they seriously try to do this, the chances are that their work will turn out to have many good features. In counselling terms, this is a 'paradoxical intervention' or 'symptom prescription' (Watzlawick, Weakland and Fisch, 1974).

Go for the jugular – that is, avoid playing safe and reproducing stale facts or theory – follow the risky, even outrageous thought, provided that it is based on your authentic experience. It can be tied into, or contrasted with, a theoretical position later.

To sum up, Goldberg's 'rules for writing practice' apply to getting started and to building up confidence and familiarity with the written word. However, the time comes when you need to give your work some structure. For help with this, see Chapter 9.

Tools for writing

One of the authors of this book writes everything in longhand, with a pen on A4 paper; the other writes directly on to the computer screen using a word-processing programme. The important thing is to use whatever method suits you best and which helps you to *do* it. As far as possible, don't let prejudice get in the way of your using whatever writing tools are useful. Basic word-processing skills can be learned readily (often from one's children) and most

---

Try this

Goldberg (1991) suggests writing freely for ten minutes on a 'mini topic' to break through obsessing thought, boredom, distractions and other kinds of stuckness. Set the time aside then 'keep your hand moving'. Here is an example of 'ten minutes on empathy'.

It's never possible, really to understand something from another person's point of view. It seems important to acknowledge that. It's like the idea of a mathematical limit, which can be reached more and more closely but never completely. It's amazing that we can even understand as much of another person's experience as we do (sometimes) and how that helps the person to understand their own experience in a new way. The first thing is to realise that each person has their own experience – feeling, thoughts, perceptions all together make up this thing – no, process, experiencing. Consciousness: trying to get into the consciousness of another person, as Pir Vilayat Khan says. Consciousness is not a popular word in psychological circles. Is it? But I believe that is what empathy is about. But it cannot be from a mischievous motive, nor even from a neutral position, one of mere curiosity. Then it is likely to become a violation of the other person. It must be benevolent, from compassion and fellow-feeling, without judgement, with respect and acceptance (that is what 'without judgement' means).

(The spelling has been cleaned up, but otherwise this is how it came.)
Try writing for ten minutes on 'Why I can't start to write'.

---

colleges now offer open access to word-processing equipment. On the other hand, it is sensible not to scorn a notebook and pen just because you enjoy being computer literate. On a recent outing to have a new tyre fitted to my car I (the one who writes directly on to the computer screen) took a notebook and pen with me so that I could continue working in longhand.

Many courses nowadays require work to be typed or word-processed, especially those within educational institutions, and virtually all those at post-graduate level. Educational institutions will have access to word-processing equipment, but check how readily available it is. It is very frustrating to want to write but not get time on a computer or be unable to print your work out. Thus, students in many disciplines prefer the convenience of having a word-processor at home.

If you enjoy all the facilities that come with a personal computer, and can afford the cost, you will find that some have very sophisticated word-processing capabilities. However, as a recent newspaper article points out, adequate word-processing can be found on much cheaper equipment. What such equipment can provide – an advance on a typewriter – is the 'ability to chop, change and re-order words at the touch of a button' (*The Scotsman*, 13 September 1996). Find out if you can use disks from your computer on the college computers; if so, you can get a good quality print-out on the college printer. Some old PCW (personal computer word-processor) systems come with an integral printer, and can be bought very cheaply second-hand.

Computerphobia

Some people have a very strong aversion to any kind of computing technology. This is a condition known as 'computerphobia' (Brosnan and Davidson, 1994). Computerphobic people are resistant to talking or even thinking about computers; they feel fear and anxiety towards them and may even have hostile thoughts about computers. Although only a few people experience this condition severely, a good number are computerphobic to an extent that may well disadvantage them from effective participation in a society where 'computer literacy may become . . . as much a necessity as reading literacy' (Brosnan and Davidson, 1994: 73). 'Computer literacy' refers to the use of a range of computerised technology, including telephone answering machines, automatic teller machines (ATMs) etc., and, most relevant here, word-processors.

What can be done to help people overcome computerphobia? Strategies focus on *attitudes* and *experience*. Attitude change may be encouraged by identifying the irrational thoughts underlying computer anxiety and helping people to a new concept of the technology and to see it as helpful rather than threatening. It has been shown that computer-anxious people expect to be bad at using the machines and so think of themselves as unable to cope. This can be changed by a guided and gentle programme of hands-on experience, starting with very simple approaches and gradually adding more skills as anxiety drops. Your college may well offer such a programme or you may find a sympathetic friend who is willing to help.

Incidentally, there are mixed findings as to gender role in computer anxiety; women are likely to be put off more by the 'masculinisation' of computers and the environments in which they are found, but women have been found to be as able as men to understand and use computers once they can familiarise themselves with them.

Writing the first essay

When you first come across the set topic for an assignment, it is useful to record your immediate reactions to it. Think, for example, of the following questions:

- What connection do I make to this topic?
- What are my first ideas and/or questions?
- What do I feel curious/what to know more about?
- What do I resist about this topic?
- What do I want to communicate about it?

We suggest that you start to write from the very beginning, so that writing becomes part of the process of essay preparation, rather than only what comes at the end. Keeping a note of whatever is sparked off when you meet the essay topic for the first time can be valuable, especially if you later lose your way in the amount of material gathered. Whether that happens or not, keep going back to your first responses and questions. Note how your ideas are developing and expanding – or running into a dead end. In this way, you can build up the final shape of the essay as you prepare for it, even if the end result is different from your first thoughts.

The story of an assignment

By way of illustration, we give a detailed account of the development of an essay, an assignment for a diploma course in person-centred counselling, from first getting the assignment to a final summary of the essay and the experience of writing it. Note that this is in the form of the sketch or plan that the course member made and is not, therefore, complete with the relevant literature references.

Assignment topic: the person-centred approach compared and contrasted with one other approach

First thoughts
- Choose Gestalt therapy – personal experience of individual and group work in that approach
- What were my experiences of that approach? How do they fit with my current themes/concerns?
- Reading about Gestalt – think of similarities and differences in comparison to the person-centred approach
- Why did I choose a p-c training course after all my experience of Gestalt?

Plan of essay
1. Introduction – explain the background to my choice of Gestalt
   - Explain my decision to train in person-centred approach – some bad experiences with Gestalt – danger of 'demolition job' (don't have an 'axe to grind')
   - Experience of preparing the assignment has given me a fresh perspective on both approaches
2. Learning by doing (experiential)
   - Current themes on the course revolve around issues of power and the core conditions: reflected in the assignment
   - In my view, the Gestalt approach seems to emphasise high levels of awareness in the therapist – 'congruent awareness' (cite personal experience)
   - Could this be seen as similar to focusing? (Gendlin, 1978)
   - Are Gestalt counsellors more challenging/powerful and less tentative than person-centred counsellors?
   - From talking to a Gestalt counsellor: the approach is constantly developing – more respect for 'defences'; more awareness of the power balance?
3. Learning from reading (body of knowledge)
   - Moving out from personal experience to ideas/theory from both approaches, and even wider to the context of humanistic psychology to which both approaches belong
   - Similarities – shared belief in the actualising tendency, overlaid with self-concept/introjected conditions of worth (this mixes the languages of the two approaches); belief that self-support/internal locus of evaluation is possible. Both stress the relationship between client and counsellor; theory can get in the way *during* counselling

■ Differences: along the lines of directive/non-directive and confrontation/acceptance. Key to difference in practice is awareness of power issue.

Writing the assignment: learning by writing

This personal account continues:

> I thought I knew what I was going to say when I started writing this essay. But the process of writing has clarified two themes for me.
>
> The first is about the *style* and *role* of the founders – the personalities of Perls and Rogers inevitably influenced their theories. Perls used 'scorn' arising from his 'irascibility', although this is not central to Gestalt therapy itself. The 'Gloria' tapes contrast the style of the two men. It is important here for me to find my own style and explore how to use what I've learned from both approaches about awareness and keeping the power balance.
>
> The second is that of *cross-fertilisation* between two approaches which share a foundation of belief. The person-centred approach has a lot to say about power and mutuality: the counsellor can be less tentative when the power balance is well monitored. Gestalt counselling uses a range of human interactions (drama, play, laughter, nonverbal communication, the body): person-centred approach is wary of some modes of expression because of concern about 'being directive' or of resorting to 'techniques and gimmicks' but a wider range of expression, beyond the verbal, is possible while still being mindful of the client's power and the right to choose.
>
> I expected the writing of the assignment to be a small part of the preparation and reading and thinking that I have been doing for weeks. In fact, the writing itself has been a crucial stage in my learning. The themes in the paragraphs above came out of the process of writing. In the end, the areas highlighted – style, power, and modes of expression – are all ones that I continue to learn about. I am back at my continuum: from my personal experience to an external body of knowledge, which itself has been the product of a complex mixture of ideas and the experiences and personalities of those who developed them.

Balance

The finished assignment needs to have a fair degree of balance amongst certain different elements. This does not mean that every element is measured out so as to have exactly the same space as any other. What it does mean is that no element is left out altogether or, conversely, is allowed to swamp the others. It is likely (depending on the exact nature of the assignment) that the following elements will be included:

1 Theoretical concepts with appropriate references.
2 Personal experience and reflection; personal views and opinion (clearly designated as such).
3 Reference to client work or practice.
4 Analysis and critique.

The box below illustrates good balance in an essay, a written assignment for a post-graduate certificate in counselling.

'Balance' in an essay

In the early years in particular, individual therapy provided a counter-point to my working life. It provided a place in which to attend to feelings, whereas I experienced my academic work as a place of intellectual expression. At this time, I had little conscious insight into my inner world of emotions. In person-centred terms I was 'incongruent' and I was suffering the effects of 'conditions of worth' in which the overt and vivid expression of powerful emotions was unacceptable (Mearns and Thorne, 1988). Before I embarked on therapy I tended to assume that I should be able to deal with my problems 'rationally'. In psychodynamic terms, I made much use of the defences of intellectualisation and rationalisation (Jacobs, 1988: 85–6). I believe that my sense of a division between the intellectual and the emotional may have been highlighted for me by virtue of the fact that my therapist trained and practised from a Gestalt perspective, an orientation well-known for its antipathy to intellectualisation (Feltham, 1995: 86–7; McLeod, 1993: 86–7; Perls, Hefferline and Goodman, 1951).

In a footnote, the writer adds:
Research evidence suggests that the theoretical orientation of the therapist or counsellor does not directly influence outcomes (variously measured) and that 'non-specific' factors, especially the quality of the relationship between client and counsellor, are more important than the particular 'brand' (McLeod, 1993: 80–1). However, this evidence is about broad patterns and is derived from extensive forms of research. It does not reveal anything about individual experiences of therapy and counselling, which can be gleaned only from intensive, qualitative analyses, of which autobiographical accounts are an example.

(Bondi, 1996)

Common errors

We end this chapter with a list of the most common errors found in course work essays. The list was supplied by a senior lecturer in counselling in a university offering a range of counselling training. Most of these errors can be eliminated simply by paying more attention to your writing and to proof-reading and editing your work before handing it in.

Most common errors in essay writing

- Unstructured, rambling essay
- Not addressing the essay title/straying from the set task
- Not striking a balance i.e. being overly personal/intellectual
- Failure to keep track of a line of thought – disjointed sentences
- Short, choppy paragraphs; or long rambling paragraphs; or *no* paragraphs
- Vagueness and repeated phrases
- Counselling and/or academic jargon
- Careless misspellings and typographical errors – omitting to proof-read
- Not building an argument or developing a line of reasoning
- Imitating (badly) academic texts you don't really understand (or outright plagiarism!)
- Relying for references on the few (out-of-date and not relevant) books you happen to have on your shelf
- Being eccentric, rebellious, 'grinding an axe'
- Assuming that the reader is familiar with abbreviations, jargon, etc
- Poor or sloppy presentation
- Being 'Pollyanna-ish' – insufficiently critical

Key Point

It is important to start writing early on the course, probably through the medium of a personal journal. Find out which tools suit you best (from pen and paper to word processor) but prepare to be flexible. Goldberg's 'rules of writing practice' help to encourage writing freely and to give a form to your writing. Keep a record of thoughts, questions and themes throughout the preparation stage, which help to shape the finished essay, which should be balanced in content.

9

Writing Takes Form

The structure or form of an essay is what makes it readable and is the framework in which you convey, by means of a logical development, what you want to say to the reader. There is a basic common structure expected for an academic essay. For some people, on some courses, it may be possible to experiment with different structures for written assignments, but it is generally not wise to do this and not until you are familiar with and adept at using the basic form. This is outlined in the box below.

The structure of an essay

Introduction − *title of the essay*
    Your interpretation of the question/essay topic and how you intend to address it
Part 1 − *main heading and sub-headings*
    Presenting your main argument
Parts 2, 3 etc. − *main headings and sub-headings*
    Developing the argument, offering alternative argument(s); give evidence for argument and counter-argument (if appropriate); cite literature, with references
Conclusion − *heading*
    Summarise points (briefly) and draw together. Tie in with your introductory statement. Be tentative rather than dogmatic, but not woolly. Indicate where further work needs to be done
Appendices (if any)
References

Language

The structure and form of the essay is filled out by the correct and appropriate use of language. We refer, of course, to the English language as that is the language that we are using and the language in which our readers will be asked to express themselves. We acknowledge, however, that English may not be everyone's first or 'cradle' tongue or their only language. Many British people are fluent in languages other than English such as Urdu, Hindi, Welsh and Gaelic. Also, a number of students come from abroad to train in counselling courses in Britain.

In this chapter, we concentrate on the use of language, and focus on clarity of expression, grammar and syntax and acceptable form, that is, avoiding language that does not recognise difference and distinction among people and groups.

Grammar and syntax

Try not to shudder at the word 'grammar'. Its definition is simple: 'a system of general principles for speaking and writing according to the forms and usage of a language' (*Collins English Dictionary*) and syntax is 'that part of grammar that treats the construction of sentences and the correct arrangements of words therein; the rules for governing sentence construction' (ibid.).

The language you use should convey your meaning clearly and unambiguously. Correct grammar and syntax are at the service of clarity, not merely rules that are imposed arbitrarily.

Written language

The written word is more formal than the spoken word. When we speak, we do not pay much attention to ensuring that our speech is grammatically correct. Speech is usually idiomatic or colloquial, but these common forms are not generally acceptable in written work. Spoken English is full of contractions – isn't, I'll, he'd, don't, I've – which need to be written in full, unless you are reporting or transcribing speech. We do not always use complete or correct sentences when speaking: correct sentence construction is essential in writing. Neither do we speak in paragraphs, which also have to be used in writing.

A *sentence* is a unit of language that makes sense on its own. It must contain a subject and a verb. In the preceding sentence, the subject is 'it' the verb is 'must contain' and the remaining words, 'a subject and a verb', are the 'objects'. That sentence has only one clause. You can tell because there is only one complete verb. A compound sentence has more than one clause, each of which must contain a complete verb. That is an example of one. Here is an example of an incorrect sentence (taken, incidentally, from printed guidelines on completing assignments!):

> The appendix is written with the latter group in mind, but it is hoped that everyone who is facing the task of writing their first assignment.

Clearly the sentence is incomplete, and something would need to be added either after the word 'that' or at the end. Can you think of how to complete the sentence so that it does actually make sense?

A *paragraph* is a collection of sentences that make up a single unit of thought. A paragraph should usually consist of more than one sentence. Should you end up with a long (and complex) sentence rather than a paragraph, it is better to split the sentence into a number of shorter ones. Good paragraphing can make the difference between a text that can be read and understood easily and one that is frustrating and difficult to comprehend.

It is not possible here to give a complete guide to correct English. If your writing is very rusty, there are a number of texts that are useful. *Plain English*, Open University Press (1982) is one. Some books, such as *Common Mistakes in English* by T.J. Fitikides (Longman, 1971) can help those who are not native speakers of English. *The Complete Plain Words* (Gowers, 1973, revised by Fraser) published by HMSO, was written to help clarify and simplify 'official' writing, and is invaluable for providing models of simple, correct, stylish usage.

Acceptable form: avoiding sexist and racist writing

In the past, the use of language has often been, subtly or openly, discriminatory against certain groups in society, most notably women and black people. In recent years, in the English-using world, this bias in language has been examined, analysed and challenged (see, for example, Miller and Swift, 1979; Swift and Miller, 1981; Lago with Thompson, 1996). Now, journal and book publishers give clear guidelines to their contributors on avoiding language which is sexist or biased against particular cultural or racial groups. This is from the *British Journal of Guidance and Counselling* in their 'Guidelines for the non-sexist use of language':

> It is assumed that writers for the *British Journal of Guidance and Counselling* do not set out to be deliberately sexist in their writings.

Rather, it is assumed that any sexism which does creep in is the result of habit, dependence on conventional (sexist) usage, or possibly on a lack of realisation that some terminologies or phrases are actually sexist.

Check that your language does not exclude or denigrate certain cultural or other groups in our society. For example, reference to 'Christian names' is inappropriate in a multi-cultural society where people have different religious backgrounds. The problem can be avoided by using the term 'first name'.

Some examples of sexist language

We cannot cover all the forms of sexist language in the space available, so will give examples only of the more obvious. For a full treatment, see, for example, Miller and Swift (1979).

1. The generic 'he'. This is when the pronouns 'he', 'his', 'him' and so on are used in such a way as to intend the inclusion of women as well as men, either when the gender of the subject is unclear or when it is neither male nor female (such as 'child'). In effect, women are likely to feel excluded. For example:

> The teacher's job here is to ensure, whether he is explaining to the children or helping them to find out for themselves, that it is possible for new learning to be integrated into the existing frame of understanding. (Stones, 1966: 367)

Ways to avoid the 'false pronoun':

i.   Change the subject to the plural if possible e.g. 'The implications for teachers are clear. They cannot satisfactorily teach . . .'
ii. Use 'she or he', 's/he', 'his or her', etc.
iii. You may be able to leave the pronoun out altogether: 'The implications are clear for teachers, who cannot satisfactorily teach . . .'
iv. It is now acceptable to use 'they' or 'their' even when the subject is singular, if it helps to avoid a clumsy construction.

2. A similar mistake is to use the term 'man' to mean all human beings, or persons. A popular television programme of the 1960s *The Ascent of Man* was followed by a book *The Descent of Woman* (Morgan, 1972) whose author had not only written a scholarly

work about human development but was also ensuring that half of the human race was not simply ignored.

3. Use of qualifiers or diminutives. It is not long ago that the term 'lady doctor' was in common use (and is still used, mainly by older people, in some parts of the country at least); nobody would say 'gentleman doctor', for it was assumed that 'the doctor' would be a man. Similarly, one might hear of a 'male nurse', for nurses were assumed always to be female. The phrase 'the girls in the office', to refer to adult women office workers, is an example of diminutive use. It is not unlike the use of the term 'boy', in some places in the past, to refer to adult black males.

Concern about sex-biased writing is comparatively recent. Therefore, you will still find texts used in counselling training which refer to 'he' and use 'man' or 'mankind' to indicate the whole human race. Even Carl Rogers, whose personal and immediate style of writing was often the antithesis of the false generic, wrote in *On Becoming a Person* (1961):

> It seems that gradually, painfully, the individual explores what is behind the masks he presents to the world, and even behind the masks with which he has been deceiving himself. (Rogers, 1961: 114)

Rogers soon accepted that such language did not fully include or acknowledge women. By 1977, he wrote the following:

> I have been greatly perplexed by the pronoun problem . . . I am totally in sympathy with the view that women are subtly demeaned by the use of the masculine pronoun when speaking in general of a member of the human species. On the other hand, I enjoy forceful writing, and a 'himself/herself' in the middle of a sentence often destroys its impact. I do not believe that a satisfactory solution will be found until someone comes up with an acceptable set of nonsexual pronouns.
>
> I have chosen to deal with the problem in this way: In one chapter all general references to members of our species are put in feminine terms, in the next chapter masculine . . . It is the best solution I could find to serve both of my purposes, an equalitarian aim and a desire for forcefulness. (Rogers, 1977: ix)

Other writers have tackled the problem differently. Mearns and Thorne (1988), in the introduction to *Person-Centred Counselling in Action*, write: 'In our British experience, however, female counsellors seem to outnumber their male counterparts; hence our general usage makes the counsellor female and, for the sake of clarity, the client is usually male.' In this case, the authors have tried to make their use of pronouns reflect the reality of practice; but it still leaves a problem for the inclusion of male counsellors. Another solution is shown in this example:

> Although humans live and adapt as do other biological creatures, one of our truly unique qualities is that we are also aware of ourselves and what we do, and we view ourselves as having a past, present, and future. (Lazarus, 1976)

Probably the best way to avoid racial, cultural and social stereotyping is to be wary of generalising, especially by assuming (often implicitly) that the standard or norm is white, male, heterosexual. As far as possible, be specific and personally relevant.

What is correct English?

Although English is a 'living language' and is therefore always changing, it is still expected, in academic writing, that words will be correctly used and correctly spelled. Some course tutors are more insistent on this than others, and the recent trend has been towards less rigidity about spelling, exact grammatical expression and word usage. For example, the words 'less' and 'fewer' are commonly used as if they were interchangeable. Correct usage is that 'less' applies to quantity or extent and is followed by a singular noun (less counselling); 'fewer' applies to number and is followed by a plural noun (fewer counsellors). Another common confusion is that between 'infer' and 'imply' – look these ones up for yourself!

An example of the increased acceptance of language usage formerly considered incorrect is the permissibility of using a 'split infinitive' to avoid a clumsy construction. To split an infinitive means to lace another word between the two parts of the infinitive of a verb. If the infinitive is 'to go' then 'to boldly go' (quoting Captain James T. Kirk of the starship *Enterprise*) is a split infinitive. Split infinitives are regularly used in spoken English largely because they often simply sound more 'natural', but are not correct form in written English. Correct written versions of the example given above would be 'to go boldly' or 'boldly to go'.

It is unfortunate that sometimes more formally educated people (perhaps in the role of teachers or academic tutors) act rather like the 'grammar police' which can discourage those who have had less formal education, or who went to school during the time when grammar and spelling were not taught because of a fear of stifling children's creativity. Tutors nearly always want to help their students to produce their best possible work, and are unlikely to want them to feel inferior because their English has been corrected. However, anxiety about a lack of formal language skills can hold a person back from submitting or even completing written work. Perhaps the best advice is to keep your writing simple and to check it over for any obvious errors of grammar or spelling. This simple act of proof-reading and correcting can make the difference between a readable, competent essay and a confused, careless submission which, although it may contain some good material, has to be redone.

It is best to use only words that you are familiar with and whose meaning you understand. The use of a good dictionary enables you to check the meaning of a word when you are unsure. It also helps you build your vocabulary as you gradually incorporate new worlds, trying each one out until you can use it fluently. Your own reading and active listening to those who use words well are the best sources. Ask about the meaning of any word that is unfamiliar to you. If you want to be sure that you are correct in your use of language, or if your tutors insist on it, a good reference book is still *The Complete Plain Words* (Gowers, 1973). English usage, has, however, changed even since 1973.

Spelling should be checked using a dictionary. If you are using a word-processor, it will probably have a 'spell check' facility which will check the spelling of each word and stop at any which the programme indicates are doubtful. The spell check should be used with caution. It does not take account of the context in which the word is used – it cannot distinguish between 'practice' (the noun) and 'practise' (the verb), for example, nor between 'their' and 'there'. It cannot pick out an incorrect word if it is correctly spelt. Thus, essays have been submitted with variously, 'locus of evaluation' and 'focus of evaluation'. And, annoyingly and sometimes amusingly, the spell check is very confused by proper names and often wants to turn them into something else, which may be appropriate or not.

Style

We do not wish to suggest that everyone should adopt the same style of writing. Rather, you need to find your own writing style. This is what gives variety and life to writing even at the level of course work. At first, however, it may be difficult to trust your own inclinations especially if you are uncertain as to whether your writing is correct in the basics. Here are some considerations regarding writing style.

It is generally not good to be dogmatic in your writing. To do so, sets you up to be criticised or challenged by the exceptions to the statements you have made. For example, the first sentence of this paragraph states: 'It is *generally* not good . . .'. In this case, the word 'generally' modifies the statement from 'It is not good . . .', since there may be a case for making a dogmatic statement on ·some occasions.

Other ways of modifying include the use of 'would' 'could' and 'might' as modal verbs; or use phrases such as 'seems to', 'as if', 'I suggest' and so on. The sense of 'making a pronouncement' is also softened by using, for example, 'often', 'perhaps' or 'maybe'. Here is an example from writing this book: at the beginning of Chapter 8 part of a sentence reads, '. . . for oneself and one's own experience are *often* the very stuff of writing' (new italics). Originally this read, '. . . for oneself and one's own experience are the very stuff of writing' (i.e. on counselling courses). The additional word is a recognition that sometimes writing on counselling courses is *not* only about one's own experience.

In part, how tentatively one writes is related to the preferred core model of counselling (MacMillan, 1993: 144). A person-centred approach, for example, is likely to be tentative and inviting, in order to avoid the danger of imposing a view on either the client or the reader. A psychodynamic approach could accommodate more interpretive or even diagnostic wording, and a cognitive approach would avoid incorporating 'irrational' statements – such as 'What she said made me feel terrible' – into the text.

Perhaps the best way to develop this style of writing is to look out for examples in the texts which you are reading. Here are some instances:

> At this point you might ask your client what he would like to achieve . . . (Dryden, 1990: 25)

> At the outset, students naturally rely a good deal on the advice and comments offered by the supervisor. (Casement, 1985: 32)

> Such utter desolation is only likely to occur, in the author's experience, in situations where a basic and extensive reorganization of self is taking place. (Rogers, 1951: 116)

Of course, one should guard against using too many modifying words and phrases, lest writing should become flabby and indecisive. It is irritating, too, to use many longer words when the meaning is clearer and the style more pleasing if fewer, plainer words are used. A student wrote: 'She was bereaved of her younger brother in the November of 1994.' Why not write, simply, 'Her younger brother died in November 1994'? Check through what you have written and remove or simplify redundant or fancy words.

Eric Berne, the originator of Transactional Analysis (TA), particularly ridiculed long-winded and largely meaningless writing by psychotherapists. He showed this in the 'spoof' title of a talk he gave: 'Away from a Theory of the Impact of Interpersonal Interaction on Non-verbal Participation' (Berne, in Steiner and Kerr, eds, 1976: 5–17). He started with 'Away from' because so many papers have titles beginning with 'Towards a . . .', and 'you wonder when they're going to get there'. Note that this also fits in with the TA approach in counselling, in which counsellors pay close attention to how their clients use language and will challenge expressions like 'I'm *trying* to write this paper', by saying, 'Why don't you stop *trying* and actually *do* it?'

Jargon

Gowers (1973: 71) defines 'jargon' as 'technical terms . . . which are understood inside [the department] but are unintelligible to outsiders'. He was referring to the language used within government departments, but counselling and its various approaches have also devised a host of technical terms: projection, transference, containing, congruence, locus of evaluation, ego states, confluence and awfulising are but a few. It is, of course, appropriate to use these technical terms in context. Be sure, however, that you understand the meaning of the term and that the context conveys this understanding to the reader.

For example, in describing the process of a small group, a student wrote: 'A lot of transference was going on.' This does not make sense as it stands. It is necessary to *describe* what happened and then point to the elements which can be understood as transference phenomena. Another example might be the misuse of 'congruence' applied to counsellor self-disclosure: 'Being congruent, I told her what it had been like when my brother died.'

Psychobabble could be thought of as the spoken equivalent of jargon. An article in *The Scotsman* (18 September 1996) quotes Adam Phillips, thus:

> Learning to talk is very difficult and it doesn't get any easier. There is a real risk that psychobabble becomes a reflex language as though people can talk about feeling anxious or narcissistic or having penis envy – *as though we all know what that means*. It is like learning a faked-up language to describe what are the most difficult things to talk about. [our italics]

American English

Many books on counselling come from the United States. This brings a two-fold problem: differences in actual words and their meanings and differences in spelling of words. Some common counselling words spelled differently in the USA include 'counseling', 'behavior', 'person-centered', 'defense'. As far as spelling is concerned, the rule is to use the American spelling when directly quoting from an American text. At all other times, use standard British spelling for English words.

Sometimes, American writers use words that differ from the equivalent British word. For example, the word 'normalcy' instead of 'normality'. In our quotation from Carl Rogers on page 90, the word 'equalitarian' *is* the word used, whereas we in Britain would use 'egalitarian'. There is a grey area here, since there is always a process of change and development in language and its usage, and it is unrealistic to expect to lock the doors against the infiltration of American English. Generally, however, it is more acceptable (and more pleasing?) to stick with British English. A good contemporary dictionary will provide the means of checking current usage.

Key Point

When writing, it is not only important to use language which is correct in terms of grammar and syntax, and fully inclusive of social and cultural groupings – but also language which is in a style both personal and in tune with your preferred counselling approach. Contain your essay in a simple and coherent form and take time to proof-read so that basic errors can be edited out.

10

Using Other People's Work

This chapter is concerned with using other people's work in your learning. Although material is now available in a variety of forms – video-tape, audio-tape, Internet pages, CD ROM for example – the main focus will be on material in print. We look at choosing what to read, how to read it, retaining what you read, making notes, and how to incorporate other people's material in your own writing.

What to read

Where do you start selecting material which might be relevant to your own learning? In the broadest sense, counselling concerns being human and relating as fully as possible to other human beings. Depending on where your interest lies and what your questions are at this stage of your journey, you may be stimulated and inspired by any area of human experience – personal relationships, fiction, movement, chaos theory, music, energy work, mysticism, biography, art, history, quantum systems, science, psychology – the list could be endless. It is most important to go to the original sources of material (works are sometimes quoted out of context) and to use the most up-to-date publications.

Within the vast arena of accumulated human experience and knowledge, you have chosen to learn in the specific area of counselling and psychotherapy, and within that you are likely to be training in a particular theoretical approach. Although we will focus on tracking down texts which are relevant to your chosen field of learning, it is important to affirm at the outset the range of material in a variety of forms that may have relevance for you and which can contribute to your learning. It is worth trusting your sense of being engaged and interested wherever it takes you. If you are then conscious of where your own learning and development is happening, it will be easier to see how it can contribute to whatever pieces of work you are asked to produce on the course.

Returning to the question of what to read, we look at four possible starting points for tracking down material:

1 Bibliographies
2 Libraries
3 Bookshops
4 Word of mouth

Bibliographies

Most courses will provide participants with a detailed bibliography or book list at the start of training. Some may issue lists of relevant reading throughout the course as new topics or assignments are approached. These bibliographies can be overwhelming. Sometimes core texts will be highlighted or books will be marked or grouped in some way to indicate their level of importance. If you need guidance, ask your tutors for direction. It may be that there are a few key texts that are required reading and it is worth finding out which texts it would be useful to buy if you will be referring to them throughout the course. It is unlikely that you will be expected to read every item, except on the shortest of bibliographies which should then make clear that they list required reading. More often these lists of books and articles are given to indicate the range of relevant material and to help you follow up particular points of interest. If you do feel overwhelmed, it may be worth asking your tutors how many of the books listed *they* have actually read. In most cases, the answer will calm you down.

Another source of information, which is easy to overlook, is the reference material given in books. If you are reading and come across a point or topic that interests you and there is a reference in the text, you can find a full description of the text in the list of references at the end of the book (or chapter) with sufficient detail to enable you to find it in a library or order it in a bookshop, if it is still in print. As well as (or instead of) a list of references, you may find a bibliography at the end of a text. This is a list of the main works consulted in the writing of the piece, which are not necessarily cited in the text.

When you are writing, you need to check whether tutors on your training course prefer specific references or are content with a bibliography. This may depend on the nature of the assignment and the level of the course. It may seem to you that bibliographies exist in order to impress others by their length, but they are useful in helping you explore other people's ideas which you come across indirectly. They can help you find your way through your own treasure hunt.

Libraries

Most counselling trainees have access to a library, either at the educational institution where the course takes place or at the local public library. It is a common experience on visiting a library for the first time to feel that everyone else there knows their way around perfectly and that only you feel totally lost, not knowing where to start. Libraries do differ in their lending habits, layout and cataloguing systems. On the whole, they make leaflets readily available near the entrance which provide basic information for new users. You can start by finding out

- opening times
- how many books you can borrow
- for how long
- what cataloguing systems are used and how to access them
- the layout of the library
- where to find periodicals, reference books, audio-visual material, past exam papers, on-line databases
- where photocopiers and study spaces are located

Finding a book using the catalogues

Many libraries now have on-line catalogues accessible by computer terminals. These are designed to be user-friendly, but if you get stuck ask someone for help. Librarians are often user-friendly, too. You can usually track items down using the author's name, title or subject heading. The computer will prompt you which one of these to type in as a 'keyword'.

Once you have found the item you are looking for (or something else of interest) note the *classmark* in full. This will be a combination of letters and numbers, according to the classification system used in the library. Then consult a plan of the library, or follow the signs to find your item.

When you have reached the right shelves, the actual text you are looking for might not be there – the catalogue might be able to tell you if the item is 'shelved' or not – but it might still be worth scanning the shelves in that area to see if anything else catches your eye since the books will be grouped by subject. If you do want to get hold of a particular item which is not on the shelves, ask at the library desk for the book to be reserved for you. You can also reserve books in many libraries by using the computer terminals. If you are computer-phobic, ask for help (see Chapter 8).

Other library services include:

Short-term loan for books in heavy demand, which may have been put on short loan at the tutor's request. The short loan desk is often located at or near the main desk. The catalogue should indicate items held for short loan only. Find out how long you can borrow these items for. It will range from a few hours to overnight or for the weekend. Ask your tutors to put any popular texts which you are having difficulty finding, on short loan (if they are not there already).

Inter-library loan for obtaining material from other libraries, such as books and articles from periodicals which are not held by your library. This service is expensive but the cost to students is often subsidised. It can take some time for the material to come through, so check how long you will have to wait before you order.

Leave yourself lots of time to track down material in the library. Items may have to be recalled from another reader or ordered from another library. Start locating material in advance of when you plan to start work, since it can be very frustrating to start your library search at the time you have scheduled for reading for an essay, and then find that nothing is available.

Bookshops

Get to know your local bookshops and you may find that a particular one becomes your favourite. It may be that you find the staff friendly and helpful; it may be a large shop with a good counselling section or it may be a small specialist shop which holds a lot of material of interest to you. Visiting bookshops can be about tracking down and buying a particular text (even if you have to order it) and it can also be for browsing and just seeing what is available and what you are drawn to. One of us, while on a counselling course, was browsing in a favourite small shop and the book that 'jumped off the shelves' was *Against Therapy* (Masson, 1989) which turned out to be just the right book to read at that particular time and which could not have been found in any other way.

As an alternative to visiting the bookshop in person, you can obtain catalogues direct from the publisher. This tells you what books are available and is particularly informative about those which have just come on the market. It is easy to order books direct – if you have a valid credit card! This is especially useful for people in more rural areas or who cannot travel to or access bookshops. The only drawback is the payment of postal charges (but offset against a trip into town?).

Word of mouth

Writing this section, I (DC) have become intrigued by how the process of selection works. Out of the immense weight of past human learning and experience, how do certain records of this end up in bibliographies or on library shelves? How do these selections change? How have I tracked down or been given things that have fed me at just the right time? A powerful part of the selection process involves other people. As I talk to friends and colleagues about a particular theme which engages me, people mention what they have found helpful in that area. I get given clues which I can follow up and sometimes I even get given the book.

I read a lot of fiction and most of what I read is recommended by friends and family or occasionally by reviews in the weekend papers. In the counselling field, I am intrigued by some books reviewed in *Counselling* (journal of the BAC). And on my diploma course I read several books which were recommended by others after we had shared personal issues and knew which books addressed the kind of questions we were interested in.

I know how often books I have read pop into my head as someone tells me about their concerns. I am also aware of the need to be tentative when mentioning something that I have liked. It may not suit the other person's interests or style and, if I have a big investment in what I am recommending, it can be hard to hear that it does not suit someone else.

But I want to be aware of and value these personal processes by which other people's work gets known and transmitted. If the sources of recommendation remain distant and authoritative, I can feel disempowered and cut off from the very ground which I am trying to explore. Someone else is mapping it out for me and I become just a consumer of learning to regurgitate it later. To digest something fully, I need to be involved in the process of following my tastes and appetite.

So I suggest that you pay attention to the way in which you come across other people's work while you are on the course. This could be structured by inviting course members to talk about what has influenced, stimulated and fed them in their learning. By such means, a group of people on a counselling course can acknowledge their role in creating the culture they share.

Two further points:

Be realistic in what you expect of yourself: when you have located all your material, ask yourself, 'Have I collected too much?' You do not have to read everything.

Keep referring back to the question. If you are reading in preparation for an assignment, keep checking with yourself:

■ am I wandering too far from my subject?
■ is my focus getting too big/too small?
■ what are my questions about this topic?

How to read

This may seem like a pointless heading since you are reading this sentence right now. But notice *how* you are reading this book. Are you flipping through it to get a flavour? Did you get here from page one and every page following, word after word? Did you choose this chapter from the contents page? Did you arrive here after looking up something in the index? Are you skim-reading just now, tasting what is presented, or are you reading slowly and deliberately, digesting everything as you go? Are you reading every word or a cluster of phrases? Can you notice your reading rhythm and when it changes? Are you calculating the time as you read, for example. 'It's taken me two hours to get this far. At this rate, I won't finish the book till the end of next week'?

These questions are about making your relationship with the book explicit. That relationship involves giving the book a chance to say what it says, as well as keeping in touch with what your needs are and whether or not they are met by this book right now.

How you read depends on what you are looking for. If you are reading core theoretical material for the first time, you may need to read slowly and thoughtfully. If you are reading around an area where you are already familiar with the basics, you may speed up and look out for comments which are new, different or expressing a particular author's point of view. With a book like this one, you might slow your reading only at a section that is of particular interest to you and skim the rest.

Learning happens inside you as you engage with an issue. If you are plodding on waiting for things to get interesting, it isn't happening! When reading becomes a task, stop and ask yourself what is going on. Is it that the text itself is boring or is something getting in the way? Maybe you should leave that book or maybe you can't give it a chance until you are less tired, or have made that phone call, or decided what you are having for tonight's meal, and so on. Do not assume, however, that if you do not understand something it must be your problem. Sometimes books are poorly written, or overloaded with jargon or obscure technical terms.

You will have noticed how many food metaphors are used about reading. Here is one more – if you get stuck, it may be that you need to digest before you can take in any more. That can mean moving away from the individual activity to some equivalent of 'after dinner conversation'. You may need to talk through with someone the ideas you have taken in, in order to aid digestion/integration. Perhaps the activity of reading may not need to be as solitary as it appears. There may be ways of sharing resources with others on the course, distributing reading round a group with everyone reporting back on what they have read and their responses to it. Try also reading aloud in a small group, followed by discussion of the passage read.

Making reading work for you

As you read, you may think, 'So-and-so said something about this issue that contradicts this point/appealed to me more/expressed it better (or worse).' How do you back track and access material which you have covered earlier? How can you help yourself retain what you are reading in a form that is useful and helps bridge the time gap between your reading and digesting rates? Indeed, how can you help yourself remain actively involved in the process of reading as you do it?

Often people find it helpful to take notes on what they have read, either as they go or after each section or chapter. The kind of notes made varies with individual learning style and with the content of what is being read.

Core material

Theory, for example, calls for clear factual notes, summarising in a form which aids your understanding. List key points by number, paraphrase in your own words or note direct quotations which capture the author's point neatly in a way which you can quote in an essay. Mark quotations clearly, to avoid unintentional plagiarism (see later in this chapter).

Supplementary reading (expanding on material which you have already read)

This may not require detailed notes at all. You may simply want to note the points where this author has a different perspective or sheds new light on something familiar.

The key thing to remember whenever you find yourself making notes on what you are reading is that *you* are in there too. Jot down your questions, doubts, reactions as you go. You could use a different coloured ink in order to distinguish your 'running commentary' from your notes on the text. Ask yourself as you read what it is that you are learning; is this helping you explore your chosen topic; is it relevant or irrelevant? Are you bored or passive or disengaged, and if so, why?

Warning Producing a beautifully neat set of notes is not in itself a substitute for (or even an aid to) learning. Pay attention to when you become a passive copier of pieces from the text, but have lost connection with the meaning. Find out what that is about. Are you distracted? Is this particular text boring you? How can you recover the feeling of being responsible for what is going on?

Making notes on your reading

Making notes can help you
- to concentrate as you read
- to keep active in the process
- to produce summaries of a theory or argument
- to remember specific points
- to have access to pithy quotes from original material
- to note your own reactions before they get lost or overtaken
- to have a record to go back to as you digest what you have read

---

Using what you read in what you write

In your assignment writing, you may need to refer specifically to things that you have read, in order to support your argument, for instance. In any case, it is essential that the source of any views, ideas or information that you have gathered from your reading should always be acknowledged. This avoids slipping into plagiarism (the unacknowledged use of another person's work) and gives the information needed for anyone else who wishes to refer to that work. The definition of plagiarism is 'stealing the words, ideas, etc. of another and using them as one's own'. The word itself is derived from *plagiarius*, a Latin word meaning 'kidnapper'. Plagiarism is nowadays regarded as one of the major prohibitions in higher education institutions and it is likely that tutors will be on the look-out for any violations of this rule.

Some of the concepts may seem to be so generally well-known that it is tempting not to give a specific reference. For example, the 'core conditions' in the person-centred approach to counselling, or the idea of 'automatic thoughts' in cognitive therapy. Not to give a reference, however, not only does not respect the originator of the ideas – in the first case, Rogers (1951) and in the second, Beck (1976) – but can lead into using technical terms in a jargonistic way, and even to a kind of 'psychobabble' (see Chapter 9). If the phrase is used frequently, it is not necessary to repeat the reference every time.

When quoting directly from a text, keep to the original spelling; for example, American texts will use 'counseling' with one 'l' which should be left as it is in a quotation. If you add any words, for instance to make a quote fit grammatically into your text, put them in square brackets [ ] to show they have been added. If you leave out any words in the middle, either to shorten the quote, or to make it fit the context, replace them with an ellipsis – three full stops . . . like this. In any case do not add or leave out words that change the meaning of the passage cited. You can emphasise a part of a quote by putting it in *italics*; but add '(my italics)' in brackets at the end to show that they are not in the original.

As you read counselling texts, look out for all of the ways in which their authors have quoted from other people's work. This is often referred to as 'citing' other people's work. The following example from MacMillan (1993) shows how this should be indicated in the text:

> Investigators acknowledge their subjective involvement in the research which is still 'objective, in the sense of making contact with a hidden reality'. (Polyani, cited in Hutterer, 1990)

Referencing

Always take a note of the source of any quotations and other references. You can do this on index cards or, more likely nowadays, note them on a computer or word-processor file. Doing this can save hours of searching for the reference when you come to produce the finished document.

What to do if you lose the reference
If, however, being human, you lose or forget to take note of a reference, try the following ways to find it.

■ Look for the book in the library catalogues
■ Look in the bibliography of a book with similar subject matter
■ Look in the bibliography of a general text on counselling
■ Ask someone else who might know
■ Look in publishers' catalogues
■ Ask your friendly local bookshop to find it on their computer
■ Try the Internet if you have access to it. Type a keyword such as the author's name into a 'search engine' and click on 'Search'. You may need to use a little ingenuity to cut down the number of matches found or to find an alternative keyword.

Forms of referencing
There are two main forms. The first is known as the Harvard system and the second is the numerical system. It is best to find out which is preferred by your course, or institution, or the publisher when an article or book is involved. In any case, do not mix up the two systems. We prefer the Harvard system, which is used throughout this book, and is probably the most widely used.

Harvard system   In the text, give the author's name and date of publication in brackets e.g. '. . . as Bion (1961) noticed . . .'. With a direct quotation, include the page number, thus: 'We *recognize* people without having to think who they are' (Bohart, 1996: 200); not 'p. 200'. If there are more than two authors the textual reference is usually given as, for example, (Watzlawick et al., 1974). At the end of the piece, list all the works referred to, alphabetically, by author's surname (last name). The names of all of the authors are given in the form of last name followed by initials. If there is more than one work by an author, list them chronologically, the earliest work first. Refer to any text which uses this method of referencing as a model.

Numerical system   In the text, number the references as you use them, and use the same number each time you refer to that work e.g. 'The theory of experiencing (25, 26) could be summed us as . . .' At the end, list the references by number. This is a rather more complex system, especially if you are giving a number of direct quotes from the same author, and it is our view that this is now rather out-of-date.

Here is the form in which you should list your references.

If it is from a book:
- name of author/editor, with initials
- date of publication, in brackets
- book title, underlined or in italics, edition or other information
- place of publication (if required)
- name of publisher

e.g. McLeod, J. (1993), *An Introduction to Counselling*. Buckingham: Open University Press.

or:

Dryden, W. and Feltham, C. (eds) (1992) *Psychotherapy and its Discontents*. Buckingham: Open University Press.

A chapter in an edited book is referenced thus:

MacMillan, M.I. (1993) 'Education and counselling', in B. Thorne and W. Dryden (eds), *Counselling: Interdisciplinary Perspectives*. Buckingham: Open University Press.

If it is from an article:

- name of author(s) with initial(s)
- date of publication (e.g. journal) in brackets
- title of article
- name of publication, underlined or in italics
- volume, number and pages

e.g. Holmes, P., Paul, S. and Pelham, G. (1996) A Relational Model of Counselling, *Counselling*, vol. 7, no. 3, 229–32.

or:

Holmes, P., Paul, S. and Pelham, G. (1996) 'A relational model of counselling'. *Counselling*, 7(3), 229–32.

For media (e.g. video):

- author or director
- date of publication in brackets
- title
- format and length
- any accompanying material

e.g. Shears, J. (producer) (1996), *Michael Jacobs in Conversation with Andrew Samuels, part II: The Political Psyche and the Plural Psyche*; Audio-visual Services, University of Leicester, VHS video cassette, 90 minutes.

Key Point

There are many ways (including the course book list or bibliography) to find material that other people have written that can inform your learning and your own written work. Pay attention to how you read and make useful notes, stored in such a way that you access them easily when needed. Avoid plagiarism and do not recycle chunks out of books. Always give a reference for any work you cite, according to the convention favoured on the course.

11

Problems, Problems, Problems

It can be useful to look at your approach to course work and study in terms of three components: study skills, study habits and attitudes. Some of the skills of studying are considered in Chapter 5, and Chapter 12 looks at attitudes to work in the context of maintaining concentration and motivation. In this chapter, we discuss work habits – how good habits can be developed which fit into, rather than conflict with, your daily life. This leads to as good a definition as any of 'time management' which is that it is an approach to organising the events of your life so that you manage your time rather than have time manage you.

Organising your work time

The majority of those who undertake counselling training have other, busy lives to lead at the same time. A balance has to be found and maintained so that the demands of one part of life do not get lost in the demands of the other. As many (perhaps most) counsellor training courses are part-time, the rest of your life may be going on as 'normal' (whatever that means) and the course work has to be fitted in as an addition.

In some ways, it is simpler to go on a full-time course (if it is feasible to do so) taking into account time, financial and family commitments. The initial upheaval may be greater, students may uproot themselves (and also their families) to new, temporary accommodation and extensively reorganise the whole fabric of their lives. This calls for, and can help to maintain, a high degree of motivation. The full-time nature of the course can mean that the weekly schedule can be envisaged from the beginning. Thus, it may be easier to stick to a weekly or daily timetable.

This highlights one important principle: *The fewer on-the-spot decisions that have to be made about whether to get down to work or not, the more energy is saved for actually getting on with it.* For example, if an initial decision is made to schedule work time every weekday evening from 7–9 and 9.30–10 p.m. (the break to enable one to watch the news or an escapist TV programme, or to see the kids to bed), the decision has only to be stuck to, not made every time.

Whether the course is full-time or part-time, you need to have some time off. Perhaps one of the main functions of time management is to give yourself permission to take time away from work, without feeling guilty. It is a good idea to work out, as far ahead as possible, when it is important for you *not* to be doing course work – this can be for pleasure or duty or both – and make a clear decision to leave those times free. In any case, plan to have some days completely free of work. For instance, you might decide to have Sundays off, either to do other things for yourself or to spend time with your family. If it feels too difficult to take the whole day off, at least leave the major part of it free of work. One common problem, especially with conscientious workers is that they feel anxious and guilty when they are not working. It is important, therefore, to make the decision about appropriate time off consciously and in an 'adult' frame of mind. This is likely to mean checking out with yourself (or with a helpful listener) what nagging voices or negative thought patterns keep bringing back those guilty feelings. They may be related to your irrational belief that you must be a perfect worker or be part of a psychological game pattern like 'Look how hard I'm trying' (Berne, 1964).

Remember it will be tempting, when you are under pressure later, to go back on the decision at certain points – 'I know I said I would come, but I've just got too much work to do' – but do resist this strongly. If you cannot keep your word to yourself regarding *not working*, it makes it harder to keep your word to yourself regarding *doing the work*. Of course, emergencies occur and some flexibility has to be allowed, but this is a good rule of thumb. Also remember that by addressing these crises in your life, you may be learning some useful strategies to offer clients.

Individual differences

It is necessary to take into account individual differences in approaches to study. One of the problems with books of this type is that they can seem to suggest a 'cookbook' or 'recipe' approach. They may also make readers feel inadequate and guilty. One may think, 'If it is as easy as the book says, how come I can't do it?'. (See Chapter 16 for some of the inside story of the writing of this book.)

Counselling trainees are likely to have some self-knowledge but the field of academic study may be a new one and you may not have a clear concept of 'myself as a studier'. It can be useful, therefore, to adopt an experimental approach with yourself as the subject. If you like schedules and timetables, by all means draw a timetable up for yourself, even put it on your wall. This is the *looking forward* approach. However, in itself it is unlikely to be enough; there has to be some monitoring of how closely you follow your schedule.

Other people find timetables are very off-putting or do not know where to start drawing one up. Perhaps your life is too changeable to discern a pattern in it, or it is too difficult to imagine how it will be affected by starting the course. It such cases, you might start by making a short note at the end of each day – or the end of each week, but this may be too long an interval – of what you have done in terms of course work in that period. From this record, a kind of base line may be established.

To be most effective, your notes should include not only a bare statement of the work that has been done, but also what thoughts and feelings you had about doing it (or not doing it), what distractions presented themselves and perhaps something about your level of concentration. The point is, however, to have enough data to be useful, not to turn making the notes into a distraction in itself.

Daily summary of work

Date:
Work done: reading
                 writing
                 preparation
                 other
Main distractions/disruptions:
Thoughts/feelings about today:
Possible next step(s):

The importance of awareness

The monitoring process should make you more aware of your study *habits* (how, when and where you work) as well as your *attitude* to the work and how that may change. It will also bring out areas in which you may need to improve on the basic *skills* needed to complete work satisfactorily. In short, being aware of what is going on for you is a first step toward sorting out difficulties when they arise.

Like all measuring or monitoring devices, keeping a record of your work and study is likely to change the thing you are monitoring. Thus, simply keeping the record may act as an encouragement to you to attend to the study requirements of the course. In other words you may well study more than if you did not keep the record at all.

Putting it off (procrastination)

The word 'procrastination' literally means 'putting it off until tomorrow' and, as we all know, tomorrow always remains in the future. There can be few people who have not said at some time, 'I'll do it tomorrow', and that may be appropriate, at the end of a long day, for example. Yet, 'procrastination is the thief of time' as the old saying has it, and a point is reached when there are no tomorrows left. Lest you are finding a rather moralistic tone creeping into the text, we would assure you that we are speaking from experience! (See Chapter 16).

The obvious solution to procrastination is to 'do it now', and it is useful to say this firmly to yourself when you notice that you are putting work off. Positively helpful self-talk may be needed to counteract negative beliefs that contribute to self-sabotaging habits like handing work in late. If you tell yourself that 'It won't be any good anyway' or 'I've never been able to do this kind of work', you will undermine your motivation to put in the effort needed. Consciously tell yourself 'I can make a good enough job of this' and encourage yourself to put in another half hour's work.

Sometimes, a more determined effort is needed to uncover and change the irrational beliefs at the root of procrastinating behaviour. Such behaviour may be serving to 'ward off uncomfortable feelings' (Dryden 1990: 36). For example, when you sit down intending to work, you may feel anxious. You may have an underlying belief that you will fail, and that this will confirm that you are a failure. Or you believe that anything you hand in *must* be perfect (see below). Or that this is such a boring task that you can put it off for a bit longer and find something more interesting to do (like watching *Neighbours* or playing computer games). These feelings may also be combined with a low tolerance for the frustration that may arise at those times when the way forward with your work is unclear, or the whole thing seems messy and confusing. At such times it is useful to remind yourself that some frustration is to be expected and to find ways – such as coping or encouraging self-talk (see Chapter 4) – to help you tolerate it.

It is true that your work will be assessed and that this may be uncomfortable for you (and some assessment procedures are more uncomfortable than others); it is true that, in the short run, it may be easier and more pleasant to avoid the discomfort and watch television, but in the long run it is easier to confront the difficulties sooner rather than later (that means *now*) and work at sorting them out. Dryden's (1990) entire text gives many pointers to combating the tendency to put work off, and could be useful if you are a serious procrastinator (and want to change).

Perfectionism

Perfectionist beliefs are often associated with procrastination. Perfectionism means being unable to complete (or even, in some cases, to start) a piece of work because of the belief that it must be perfect. This may especially affect those who did well in school and were valued or praised for it. Check out whether you have this kind of inhibiting belief. It shows itself, for instance, in continuing to read and 'research' for an essay long after it is time to get down to the writing. Sometimes, one convinces oneself that a particular book or article must be obtained before the writing can be started. Clearly, as no one can produce a *perfect* piece of work, the work will never be done.

Similarly, not wanting to give in work that is 'below standard' or 'doesn't do me justice' prevents work being finished. Who is setting these standards and are they realistic? Underlying the notion of 'doing oneself justice' there is often, again, a perfectionist tendency, and, at the same time, a fear of failure. A more psychodynamic way of looking at it, would be to consider the underlying problem of 'letting go' – in this case, letting go of your production, the essay. What might be behind your withholding? Again, this might be something you could choose to work on in your personal counselling.

Of course, it may be helpful to find out what standards can realistically be expected. It is a salutary reminder that most course essays are read once (often in some hurry) by one tutor and are then consigned to a file and that you may rarely, if ever go back to it again! Talk to course tutors; ask if you can submit a trial essay for feedback. Ask if some examples of good work can be given to you.

It can also help to talk to colleagues on the course, as long as you trust each other to be honest about the issue. As trainees in counselling (or counselling skills), you will probably be familiar with the 'yes – but' game (Berne, 1964); we all come up with excuses why we 'cannot' find time. Remind yourself that 'Achievement, does not, except by arbitrary definition, relate to your intrinsic worth' (Ellis and Harper, 1975). Yet, in the end, you have to go by the motto 'just do it'.

Distraction (or, housework never seemed so attractive)

Procrastination is aided and abetted by distraction. Real distractions do occur – it is impossible always to shut out all of the rest of life. Many returners to education, and especially to counselling training, are women, who are particularly prone to distraction from children and other household things. (Yes, it *can* happen to men, too.) A danger sign, however, is when the housework, or mowing the lawn, say, actually becomes both urgent and attractive, and simply must be done before you can settle down to work.

Meredeen (1988) categorises distractions according to four senses – visual, auditory, physical discomfort, smell. He provides a good general check list of suggestions. These include working with one familiar picture in sight rather than many flashy images; watch out for eye-strain and ensure good lighting, find the right chair for you and choose a place with suitable or adjustable temperature and ventilation. Some people like to study accompanied by background music, but noise can be the worst distraction – especially when it's someone else's. Other people's smells can be a problem, too, but mature students (which counselling trainees tend to be) who live at home may be less subject to the neighbours cooking curry or cabbage.

You will encounter your own particular distractions. For one of the authors, a perennial distraction is the habit of compulsively reading any printed material within sight, including the advertising on the mouse mat, and (shameful confession this) the disastrously distracting discovery of the solitaire game on the computer!

Anxiety

A great deal of anxiety, consciously and unconsciously, can be engendered by the prospect of writing an essay. Anxiety may perhaps be the underlying factor beneath all of the above difficulties; or, rather, they may represent strategies to avoid the anxious feelings brought on by essay-writing. A psychodynamic view of essay anxiety is given in Barwick (1995). Although much of this piece would be of interest only to those on a psychodynamically-oriented training course, parts of Barwick's analysis would make sense to a wide range of trainees. He categorises, for example, some of the subjects of his study into three groups: the non-starters, the non-completers and the non-exhibitors. A characteristic of a non-starter was seeing 'no point' in writing the essay; indeed the pointlessness might be taken to the extreme of committing 'educational suicide' (Barwick, 1995: 567), if the person never actually started any writing at all. Non-completers may protect themselves against a sense of loss associated with separation from the essay which, it is felt, will mean the loss of the feelings attached to it (Barwick, 1995: 569). Non-exhibitors are perhaps unwilling to take an independent stance (associated with growing up and leaving home) and are likely to produce essays (if they do so at all) which 'can't see the wood for the trees' – clogged with too much detail and facts but with no thread of critical thinking running through them.

Essays may be seen, by all three groups, as 'persecutory' and devoid of feeling or sensitivity. The perception in the group which Barwick studied (A' level college students) was that there was 'no place for feelings'. It is likely that this perception would not be so marked in a group of trainee counsellors: after all, there is likely to be a place for feelings on a counselling training course, though perhaps that place is not seen as residing in the writing of essays.

At least, if it is possible to talk about course members' feelings of essay anxiety, they may be rendered more manageable and less debilitating.

Another uncomfortable underlying feeling may be one of shame. Again, this feeling may exist at a sub-conscious level. Perhaps you have felt ashamed (or been made to feel ashamed) in the past, in school or over some work you did that was not considered good enough. This can be translated into thinking (irrationally) that you are not good enough at writing or speaking out in the group, thus you tend to hide your work from public view.

Dyslexia

Dyslexia is a particular difficulty which affects a number of people. It is associated primarily with difficulties in reading, writing and spelling. However, the term covers much more than this. Being dyslexic can involve problems with short-term memory, visual perception, sequencing and spatial awareness. Tasks such as filling out forms, dialling telephone numbers, remembering lists and following directions, as well as dealing with written language, can all be problematic. Often there is a marked discrepancy between an individual's overall ability and the problems encountered with specific forms of tasks.

Learning skills can be severely affected by dyslexia. It can take a long time to read text and it may be difficult to summarise and memorise information. Handwriting may be unclear, spelling poor and there may be problems with note-taking and expressing ideas in written form. It can be difficult to organise work and to maintain concentration. The following strategies can help people with dyslexia find a learning style that suits their needs:

Multi-sensory learning
Speak – read notes aloud; explain ideas to a friend
Hear – listen to books and lectures on tape; listen to yourself talking aloud
See – create spider diagrams (Buzan, 1982) and wall charts, use colour to highlight points; visualise images associated with topics
Write – practise organising thoughts by writing them in sequence; condense a topic on to a single page

Overlearning
- Approach material in a number of different ways
- Go over points repeatedly to move them from short to long-term memory
- Avoid overload: concentrate on one task at a time

There are resources that you can use if you are dyslexic. These include:

- a national listening library with taped texts
- reader service, screen readers
- visual assistance: tinted overlays, glasses, full spectrum light
- spell checkers, word-processors, dictaphones, proof-reading service

Information on all of these should be readily available from the Special Needs Adviser (or equivalent) at the higher education institution where your course is located. There may also be funds available for support and even for an assessment of the condition of dyslexia, if that has not already been done. The institution may have a policy on extension of essay deadlines, giving more time in examinations and so on. Most higher education institutions have experience of students with dyslexia and have resources available and policies in place to support such students. The course tutors or the student handbook, for example, can tell you who to go to for information and help. It is then important to make sure your tutors know of any arrangements which are made, to ensure their active support.

Good study habits

Most problems can be minimised by encouraging good study habits for oneself. Habits are to do with the 'when', 'where' and 'how' of study work.

When?　From your daily notes, you should be able to pick out some times that are likely to be most free from distractions. Try to match the kind of work you do to your mental and physical state at particular times. For example, if you are alert and clear-thinking in the morning, you may plan to write at that time. Other times may be better for reading or sorting out notes. At odd times, even in the bath, you can get into the habit of letting thoughts about course work turn over in your mind. Do not let these turn into negative thoughts, however.

Look out for times that you can use for working at either end of the day: early morning and/or late at night are often freer from disturbances. Again, fit the time in with whether you are a 'morning person' or a 'night owl'. Finally, do not despise shorter units of time. Much useful work can be done in as little as half an hour – for example: read a short article or book chapter; check through a book index; make notes for a possible essay plan; try out a writing exercise (see Chapter 8).

Where?   Try to locate a place which can be reserved for you to work in. The best situation is one where you can keep your books, writing equipment, perhaps your tape recorder, all to hand and have a good surface (desk or table) to work on and a comfortable, supportive chair. Make sure that the lighting is adequate and suitable. You need a good level of light, without glare or reflection off a computer screen. It's ideal if you have such a location in your home, but it may be necessary for you to settle for somewhere like the college library, or where the word-processing equipment can be found.

Once you have found, or set up, your 'spot', *go there only to work* and only *work* when you are there. This is a kind of self-conditioning, which helps avoid dithering about 'deciding' to work. At the time or times you have previously identified, go there, sit down, open the book or whatever and you have started. Conversely, when it is time for you to take a break, get up from your chair and leave, have a cup of tea or water the plants, then return to the work position.

Individual circumstances, life, family, etc. can make it difficult to achieve ideal conditions. Indeed, the search for ideal conditions can itself be a distraction (and a form of perfectionism). You can become able to work in *good enough* conditions, although what is good enough will vary from person to person. In any case, ideal conditions for studying do not, in themselves, get the work done or ensure high quality. Yet decent work conditions do help, and it is important to be clear about this should you have to assert your needs for space and time to work to the people in your life.

How can you work more effectively? Detailed guidelines on written assignments are to be found elsewhere in this book (see especially Chapters 8, 9 and 13). This is a more general response for those who give up the need to appear perfect.

Allow enough time for the work to be done, but not too much. Some people do work more effectively when a deadline is in sight. You will learn when things take longer than expected – such as finding books in the library, reading that important article or struggling to find the right words to express what you are thinking. You need to be willing to put up with a certain amount of inconvenience and to build up some self-discipline. Allow yourself to become engrossed in the work and even get carried away a little, but always remember that incomplete or not-submitted work does not count, whereas a good enough piece of work, with honest effort put in to it and then let go, is what serves the purpose.

Key Point

Some common difficulties arise from perfectionist-thinking which can lead to procrastination and the inability to complete assignments. Essay anxiety may need to be recognised and managed, and a realistic sense of standards is essential. Seek help for special needs such as dyslexia. Good study habits help avoid some of the problems that interfere with effective course work.

12

Motivation, Concentration and Writing Block

In the previous chapter we have looked at some behavioural and cognitively based ways of tackling difficulties with work. At times, however, the difficulties seem to be more pervasive and harder to pin down. In this chapter we look at problems concerning *motivation, concentration* and that peculiar form of paralysis known as *'writing block'*.

Motivation (again)

Walking back home from the shops, one of the authors was thinking about motivation and what she would like to say about it. She recalled mentioning 'motivation' previously (Chapter 1) and, on reaching home, re-read it. The aspect of motivation highlighted earlier, 'that which incites to action', is connected with *intention* and *purpose*. It is likely to be necessary to revisit this motivation from time to time, to remind yourself of your purpose in undertaking the course in the first place and keeping that intention before you through the difficult times.

Yet, day-to-day motivation and encouragement is also needed. It is useful to make a list of what you need to do and to set a target for the day or period of study. Beware, however, of trying to be too heroic and setting over-ambitious targets. Being consistently unable to meet your own targets is discouraging, to say the least, and it is encouragement that is needed.

It is important to find an incentive for getting the work done, e.g. 'When I've finished this I can watch that video', or whatever is your preferred reward. Make sure that you give yourself the promised reward when the work has been done. Do keep a level head about it and neither punish yourself for perceived failure, nor be lax and self-indulgent (which is really being dishonest with yourself). Perhaps the essential reward is an honest appreciation of yourself for work done to the best of your ability under the circumstances. Consider, too, that this form of behavioural self-rewarding may be a strategy that could be of benefit to some of your future clients.

Concentration

Concentration is as important in writing as it is in counselling. It is to do with the ability to give full attention. It is popularly thought that the full adult attention time span is about thirty minutes. In fact, concentration can be maintained for longer than this (ask any experienced counsellor), but the ability to concentrate may need to be developed. In any case, counsellors in training, no less than students of other disciplines, sometimes have difficulty in concentrating for any length of time and may also find it hard to summon up the motivation they once felt for getting on with their study tasks or sticking to their schedule.

Do not ignore possible physiological reasons if your loss of concentration is severe or lasting. Are you getting enough sleep? Proper nourishment? An appropriate amount of recreation and exercise? If you are lacking in any of these respects, do what you can to remedy the situation, and you may well find that concentration and motivation become much less of a problem. Sometimes the difference between those who get through a demanding course and those who do not, is not that the former have greater academic ability but that they are more able to maintain their stamina and keep their nerve.

Consider, also, having a physical check up from your doctor. A counsellor colleague who became aware of a complete lack of motivation for his counselling practice and who suspected 'burn-out' (although that did not make logical sense to him) consulted his physician who diagnosed that he was, in fact, suffering from an atypical form of pneumonia. This is not intended to frighten any reader but merely to point out the possible dangers of self-diagnosis, especially by people used to psychological ways of thinking! Clinical conditions such as acute anxiety and depression also impair concentration (amongst other mental faculties). This may seem obvious, especially to trainee counsellors, but it is important to keep in mind the possibility. For more on this, refer to *Medical and Psychiatric Issues for Counsellors* (Daines et al., 1997).

Mild or temporary difficulty in concentrating

Perhaps it is better to use the term 'difficulty in concentrating' rather than 'loss of concentration' because concentration is not a *thing* that can be lost. Rather it is a dynamic mental process (or a 'psychological faculty') that can become impaired. Concentration problems are usually first noticed when your attention starts to wander. Reading the same paragraph over and over, realising that you have been thinking of next year's holiday for some time or finding that your mind flits from one task to another, all indicate difficulty in concentrating.

Whenever you notice that this is happening, you can try out several different measures:

1 Take a break; leave your desk or wherever you are working and do something else for a short time, such as take a short walk, or do the washing up. It is usually better not to do anything that requires using your mind, such as reading.
2 After a short break, change to some other form of working: from reading to writing, say, or the other way round. If your energy is low, a more mechanical task, such as noting references for future listing, can more easily be done.
3 Become more active in your studying. For example, ask yourself some questions about the passage you are reading and note down the answers.
4 Give attention to whatever it is that is distracting you. You may decide that whatever it is needs to take priority: so, make that phone call; write the letter to your insurance company, or whatever task keeps coming into your mind.
5 Temporarily change your place for working. This seems to contradict our previous advice that one place be kept only for working. What we are suggesting is a temporary change to break a period of low concentration. If you normally work at home, try going to the library for a change. Some writers like to

work in a local café, if you can find one where you will not be unwelcome if you do not keep ordering buns (see, for example, Goldberg, 1991). Long (or even short) train journeys can be utilised. One of the authors worked out the plan for revising a chapter in the train between Dundee and Edinburgh.

Developing the ability to concentrate

It is possible to develop the ability to concentrate. One way, now being followed by a growing number of people, is to practise a form of meditation. Whatever method is followed, many find that the practice helps them become more aware of their own mental processes and more able gently to stop the mind from wandering. Meditation can be seen as a sort of exercise for the mind and, in order to bring benefits, the exercise has to be regular and disciplined. As Le Shan (1974: 15) puts it, 'Training and tuning the mind as an athlete tunes and trains his body is . . . one of the basic reasons that this discipline increases efficiency in everyday life.'

A simple (but not easy) example of a meditation exercise is 'breath counting'. Here, you count the exhalations of your breath from one to four and then back to one again. That's all. Just pay attention to your breath and count. Of course, your attention will wander. When that happens, gently bring yourself back to 'one' and start again. Le Shan suggests starting with fifteen minutes a day, but you would still find some benefit from ten minutes. Some other approaches to meditation are taught formally, such as Transcendental Meditation (TM) and Zen Meditation (*zazen*). If you want to try out one of these methods, it is better to have some formal instruction (see, for example, Jiyu-Kennett, 1989). Games and sports are also useful for training concentrative powers.

With practice, you can also increase your attention span. If you find that you habitually break off work after about twenty minutes, deliberately increase your period of working to twenty-five minutes, then thirty minutes, and so on, before you have a break. Remain conscious of when you are unable to maintain concentration and allow a break without recrimination.

Will power and self-discipline

The idea of 'will' is often quite a negative one – ' a conception of something stern and forbidding, which condemns and represses most of the other aspects of human nature' (Assagioli, 1974: 10). It is more helpful to think of 'will' as that mental function which enables us to accomplish what we set out to do. This cannot be done without some effort on our part. Each time we make that effort (however small) and complete the task we set out to do, our will is strengthened or developed. Conversely, whenever we make a conscious decision and fail to carry it out, we risk losing will, and diminishing motivation and sense of purpose.

A simple exercise, 'Decision Practice', which builds up the will is described by Reshad Feild (1985: 115–16). Before going to bed, decide on some small task that you will carry out the next day. Visualise yourself carrying out the task in every detail, and make a clear, conscious decision to complete the task early next day. When next day comes, confirm your decision and carry out the task in every detail, affirming, when finished, that the task is complete.

For example, one of the authors writes: I needed to phone my bank to stop a cheque. I had already put it off for two days. Last night I made the decision to do the task this morning. I visualised looking up the book for the bank's telephone number, getting my cheque book with the relevant details before going to the phone, dialling the number and imagining what I would say to the bank employee. The task would be complete when I had the information I wanted and had hung up the phone. This morning, I almost 'forgot' to do it again (I dislike communicating with banks!) but I recalled my decision of the night before and carried it out.

It is largely a matter of individual preference whether you choose to tackle difficulties with writing and general academic work by using visualisation-imagery techniques (to develop will) and meditation skills (to develop concentration); or opt for a more cognitive approach, which uses structured self-talk to counteract irrational beliefs and self-defeating behaviour. Of course, it does not have to be one or the other, and, indeed, there is much overlap between the approaches.

Writing block

What do we understand by the phrase 'writing block'? We use it to mean being really *stuck* in the process of writing. Words cannot be found to express thoughts; indeed, thoughts themselves do not arise or are incoherent and scattered. True writing block occurs only when all practical solutions have been tried, and the advice about work location, avoiding distractions and so on has been followed. It does not seem to stem from lack of motivation; more often motivation is almost *too* great and pressure to do the work feels overwhelming. It almost certainly will not help remove the block simply by 'trying harder'. If you have already tried the ways outlined in the previous chapter to overcome difficulties, it becomes necessary to stand back from the work and explore the 'stuckness' or block and what it means for you at this time.

We have found it fruitful to think of writing block as a parallel to 'stuckness' in the counselling process. Similar questions arise for the blocked writer as for the counsellor in a stuck process: Why can't I think of what to say next? What might this say about me and my relationship with the client (e.g. in counter-transference terms)? What might it say about the client's experience? Mearns (1995: 96) defines stuckness as 'a state . . . when the client does not appear to be moving, preparing for movement or consolidating after movement'. Like this stuckness, writing block is also a 'multi-faceted phenomenon'. The following questions, adapted from the exploration of therapeutic stuckness in Mearns and Thorne (1988: 135), help to explore writing block:

1. *Am I really blocked or am I misperceiving the process through my own impatience or because I expect my writing to move in different directions from what is happening just now?*
   Perhaps you have underestimated the amount of time needed for a piece of work, especially at the 'incubation' stage (see below) and interpret this as a block. Or the writing may not be progressing according to the plan you have made, particularly if it is very detailed and, again, it seems like you are blocked. In this case, you may need to loosen up and let the writing 'go its own way' for a time. You can check back with the plan later, and either modify it, or edit the writing.

   Writing about the therapeutic process, Mearns (1995: 97) reminds us not to expect 'steady and even . . . movement'. The writing process, also, frequently contains some periods when no movement appears to be happening (see below). Just as 'stillness and stuckness before a major change' can be a feature of counselling, so a block in production may mark a necessary (but frustrating) stage in the process of writing. Of course, the block may mean something else, but at least you might as well think of it in a positive way in the meantime instead of 'catastrophising', that is, imagining that this block is an absolute catastrophe.

2. *How might a trusted friend or observer see my process at this time? (In therapeutic stuckness, it is important to ask how the client sees it.)*

   A different perspective may give you some insight into the meaning of the block for you at this time. As you talk it out with the other person, looking at your feelings, the work itself, what it is like to be stuck, and so on, you may find that the block becomes loosened and you can begin to work again.

3. *What is the source of my block?*

   The source may lie in the *writing task*, the *writer* or the *relationship* between them, i.e. the process of writing and the meaning of the block. The writing task may have reached a dead end. Perhaps the task has not been properly understood, and so steps have to be retraced. Too little material may have been gathered – not enough reading or research has been done. Or too much material has been gathered, making it difficult to organise especially if you are reluctant to discard any of it.

   The writer (yourself) may be 'burnt out', exhausted and unable to make the judgement that you need to take some time out. Emotional factors, such as anxiety about the writing and fear of failure, or emotions related to what is happening in the rest of your life, may be interfering with your thought processes, and will need to be dealt with first. You might be blocking yourself by the way in which you think of the writing work as a chore or imposition from the course or tutors. Experiment with the thought that the essay is an opportunity for you to demonstrate your learning, a chance for genuine reflection and possible discovery. Can you find a way to acquire a sense of ownership of the writing?

4. *What is the meaning of my block at this time?*

   The following are possible sources of meaning: You may be 'reluctant to risk progress made by going further' (Mearns and Thorne, 1988: 135). If you have completed a particularly neat piece of writing you may be unwilling to risk losing it as it may have to be 'sacrificed' for you to move further in your writing.

   If you experienced an 'earlier and profound movement' in your writing – like completing a marvellous 'A' grade essay –

the paradoxical effect of this can be to block you from further writing. One of the longest-lasting writing blocks of recent times may have been that of the novelist Harold Brodkey, an acclaimed short story writer, whose first novel took twenty-seven years to deliver. *The Runaway Soul* (1991, New York: Farrar, Straus and Giroux) was 835 pages long and received mixed reviews.

There may be deeper meanings for yourself and your life which need to be examined. Perhaps if you were to go on with this work it might lead you into new and far-reaching insights about your life situation with fearful implications for change. Writing about the therapeutic relationship, for example, may show you some difficult feelings about important relationships in your own life. You may come to realise that you have not fully made some important transition, perhaps even the very transition into the training course and all it implies. If you are 'fearful of being fully present' either in your counselling practice or as the writer of an autobiographical piece or a case study, a writing block can allow you to avoid the scary possibility.

Finally, just as therapeutic stuckness may indicate a collusive pattern between client and counsellor 'unable to face bringing the relationship to a close' (Mearns and Thorne, 1988: 137), perhaps your writing block may even mean that you need to face up to the possibility of withdrawing from the course. If this is the case for you, you may not be able to move on without fully acknowledging the possibility of withdrawal and deciding either to do so, or to recommit yourself to the course. Remember, however, that 'acknowledging the possibility' of withdrawal is not the same as assuming that you must do so or that you may be thrown off the course.

The creativity cycle

Some knowledge of the process of creativity is useful in understanding what happens in enterprises which have some creative content, such as writing (even writing to fulfil course requirements) and counselling (MacMillan, 1993). Neville (1989, Chapter 6) describes a creativity cycle with four phases: *preparation, incubation, illumination* and *verification*.

Preparation   for writing is likely to take up a fair amount of time. It includes all the reading, note-taking, planning, and so on. By these means, in the preparation phase, as Neville puts it (1989: 166), is established 'a ground of data which can be processed consciously and unconsciously'. During this phase, also, we 'establish a mental set' or frame of mind in which one not only 'psyches oneself up' to do the work, but also begins to form a number of questions around the topic itself. Questions can be as general as 'What do I want to say about this topic?' or 'What was it like for me to feel completely accepted?' to specific questions like 'What did Freud say about transference and how is that different from current ideas?' As your own questions form and ideas begin to emerge in response, they lead you into the next phase.

Incubation   is like 'sleeping on it'. In relation to writing, this may last only a short time or it may go on for what seems like forever. Yet that time may be important especially if one becomes blocked after the preparation phase. The incubation phase can feel very uncomfortable.

> Anyone who has taken time over writing an essay will recognise the phase. There appears to be nothing left but a confused idea-feeling which defies any attempt to give it shape. (Neville, 1989: 168)

This phase is one of standing back, 'stopping' thinking, allowing daydreaming, reverie – perhaps while engaging in some practical activity, such as washing up, potting plants, taking exercise, having a shower – letting what we know or want to say 'come through'.

Illumination   is the phase when things start to become clear for us. Ideas may come quickly, sometimes too quickly to be put into words. There may be fleeting images, metaphors, phrases, half-remembered references to something that seems to connect with this writing. It is a good idea to have a notebook or audio recorder ready at this time to note ideas that can fade as rapidly as they become clear. A good example of allowing a period of incubation to be followed by illumination is when we 'start an essay with only a vague feeling of what it is we want to express' (Neville, 1989: 173) which is the antithesis of starting by making a detailed plan and following it through.

Both methods are valid – 'planning' and 'starting with a vague feeling'. Different people may prefer one or the other, or the same person may need either method at different times. Sometimes a well-prepared plan just doesn't come together or flow, and a writing block may be the result. How can things have gone wrong with such a good plan? It is then that courage (some might say, faith) is needed to abandon the plan to follow the 'vague feeling'. Yet, as Neville says, 'How can I know what I think until I hear what I say?' (1989: 173) or, we might add, until I read what I write? Thus, a free-association type of writing can lead from the incubation phase into the phase of illumination as the ideas take form. But this is not the end of the work.

Verification   means to check over what has been written, to verify the content (with reference to the literature or research) and to put it into proper grammatical form and structure. Included in this stage is proof-reading, checking for errors in typing, checking your references, checking spelling (see also Chapter 9). You should also ensure that the essay meets the assignment criteria, and generally tidy up – cutting out redundant parts and rewriting any clumsy sentences. This is the process of editing. Consider, also, if your written work is as well presented as it can be. If possible, it can be a good idea to ask a friend to read it over and make constructive comments. This stage is an essential one; it may make the difference between an essay containing lots of good ideas, but being unreadable; or an essay that makes a pass but misses its potential for distinction.

Key Point

Developing the ability to concentrate, maintaining motivation and exercising will power and self-discipline are all factors in getting work done. Despite all efforts, however, a 'writing block' may occur, and at such a time, a knowledge of the creative process may help you explore the meaning of the block and lead to its release.

13

Writing About Practice

An important element of any course in counselling is counselling practice. The word practice derives from a Greek word meaning 'fit for action'. It can convey two meanings in the context of being on a counselling course. We can talk about practising before the main event, like a pianist practising before a concert. In this sense, you practise when working with your colleagues on the course, perhaps in small groups or in threes with the roles of client, counsellor and observer, perhaps using audio- or video-tapes which can be reviewed together with feedback being given. A second meaning of the word practice is 'actual performance' or the exercise of a profession. Some counsellors will describe their work by saying they are in private practice, that is exercising their profession of counselling in a private rather than an institutional setting. These two meanings of the word are not necessarily easy to distinguish 'in practice'.

Counselling courses should create opportunities for all practice to be made visible and to be reflected upon. This is easier to arrange within the context of the course than it is with clients. On the course there is usually explicit agreement among the participants in practice sessions about how the experience will be reflected upon, say by reviewing tapes together or making time available for feedback from each person.

Making visible and reflecting upon work with clients which takes place outwith the course requires different methods. Some reflection may take place during the supervision opportunities presented on the course. Often, courses include assignments on practice with clients as part of the assessment programme. These may take the form of an analysis of a taped session with a client and/or a case study on work with a client over several sessions. This chapter focuses on such pieces of writing about your practice and will concentrate on work with clients rather than colleagues.

Reflecting on work with clients

All practising counsellors reflect on their work most obviously in supervision, but also when writing notes after sessions and in reviewing tapes of sessions. Keeping a written record after each meeting with a client is a great help in reflecting on the process of the work over time. The box below gives some ideas of what can be useful to record in case notes. At various times in a counsellor's professional development, opportunities (or demands!) for writing more formally about practice emerge, for example during all stages of counselling training, or when applying for BAC accreditation. The ability to reflect upon your work in writing will be a useful skill to have in your counselling career.

Notes on client sessions

Details: Date/Time/Duration of meeting
            Reference letters or numbers (to preserve the client's anonymity)
            Session number

Notes: Your understanding of the client's process
          Your interventions and their relevance in this session
          Your experience of this encounter
          The relationship with the client and its dynamics

Draw on your theoretical knowledge to inform your reflection. You may not focus equally on all of the above areas after every session, but over time you would expect to consider each aspect.

Any part of the assessment process on a training course can arouse anxiety about your performance being evaluated or 'judged'. Assignments which concentrate on your work with clients can heighten these fears because working with clients goes to the heart of the purpose of being on a counselling course. It may feel easier to accept that you find it hard to write about theory than to accept difficulties in writing about practice.

Writing about your work can feel like an impossible task. How can the depth, texture and nuances of what happened in an hour of intense relating with another person be conveyed in a form that will do the reality justice? Not only can the task feel impossible, but even to try may feel detrimental to the experience itself. It can also feel irrelevant to theorise about an experience which may have felt complete in itself at the time. If any of these points resonates with you, have a look at what that implies. It will be useful, in approaching the task of writing about your practice, to get a sense of what any resistance you feel may be about.

The aim of counselling training is to assist the development of reflective practitioners who can account for what they do. At times, maybe especially in training, theory and practice can feel very far apart. It can be tempting, while learning theory, to ask 'What does theory tell me about my experience with this client?' Such a question carries the uneasy implication that the complexity of experience with a client is being constrained by trying to fit it to theory. It might be helpful to turn the question round: 'How does my experience with the client illuminate my understanding of theory?' Perhaps such reflection can only be done outwith the session; it may be that theory can only be present in a session to the extent that it has been fully integrated. Such integration will be aided by reflecting on theory and practice together, whether this happens as you write notes after a session, in supervision or in writing about your practice for an assignment.

Counsellors reflect on their work in a variety of ways. It is important to recognise that the act of reflection itself will have an impact on the relationship with the client. Many counsellors, especially when in training, will recognise having a feeling of heightened anticipation about the next session with a client after a particularly useful supervision session, only to remember that it may not be appropriate, in terms of where the client is, to bounce into the next session full of your own fresh insight! It can help to pay attention to the effects of your reflection on yourself, for it is through you that these effects will be carried into the relationship. You may have revisited strong emotions after the session and explored them more deeply than when you were with the client: how will that be for you when you are next with your client? You may find yourself 'creating a narrative' of your experience of the client as you examine your work in supervision: do you feel closer to or further away from you client's reality as a result?

While reflection on your work is necessary, it will also affect you and therefore your relationship with your client and this aspect needs attention. In any piece of writing you do on your practice, it will be important to keep the language as personal and connected to the experience as possible. There is a risk of objectifying the client as you reflect on your work, perhaps especially in sustained written pieces of work such as case studies. See the box below for some thoughts on this.

Some thoughts from a course tutor on the impact of writing a case study on the therapeutic relationship

In thinking about writing a case study I am aware of many of the dilemmas which confront the writer about the nature of case study writing. It is not just the ethical concerns of whether or not the therapist informs the client which preoccupy me but how the very act of writing itself makes the client the object of the investigatory experience rather than the subject. This may place him/her *out there* rather than *in the relationship*, and yet it is within the potential transitional space of the holding therapeutic relationship that I believe the therapeutic work is done. I am also sensible of the critique of the feminist movement of the seventies which alerted us to the way in which men and women, but especially women, had become 'objects' of research within the social and psychological research paradigm. Indeed, the word 'case' itself is problematic, implying an objective relationship to what is being written. The case study discourse thus assumes a pseudo-scientific voice as if the writer *knows* what is happening in the therapeutic process. The very act of writing and presenting the case study in an orderly and systematic form gives the encounter between therapist and client a coherence and clarity which belies the messiness and uncertainty of this most peculiar of experiences. (Judith Fewell, 1996)

When approaching a sustained piece of writing on your work with a client, it may be helpful to ask yourself 'Who am I doing this for?'. Where is the balance between your needs, for example to complete an assignment or be accredited by BAC, and those of the client with whom you wish to be as effective a practitioner as possible? These questions invite you to clarify the parts of the process of reflection which are yours to hold, and the parts which may belong in the relationship. For example, if you are asked to resubmit a case study on your course, you may feel angry/disappointed/hurt about this. It will be crucial, in that case, to find the support you need to separate out the feelings which belong with you from those which belong in the relationship with your client before you next meet.

Confidentiality and ethical considerations

Confidentiality is of central importance in the counselling relationship. The BAC *Code of Ethics and Practice for Counsellors* (1996) states: 'Confidentiality is a means of providing the client with safety and privacy. For this reason any limitation on the degree of confidentiality offered is likely to diminish the usefulness of counselling' (B.4.1). In the light of this, it may be asked whether writing about your work with clients in a form that will be seen by more people than, for example, your supervisor should be done at all?

Section B.4.13 of the Code of Ethics and Practice states: 'Any discussion between the counsellor and others should be purposeful and not trivialising.' The purpose of reflecting on your work, whether in discussion or in writing, is to aid your development as a reflective and effective practitioner. In the long term this aim will serve your clients well and therefore seems to answer the question posed above. In the short term, the impact of such reflection on the boundaries of confidentiality with individual clients needs attention.

The Code of Ethics and Practice gives two options which are relevant to confidentiality when writing about practice. 'Special care is required when writing about specific counselling situations for case studies, reports or publication. It is important that the author either has the client's informed consent, or effectively disguises the client's identity' (B.4.12). Your decision on whether to seek consent or disguise your client's identity is likely to be influenced by your theoretical approach to counselling. Different approaches will have different perspectives on issues such as the client/counsellor relationship and the place of the counsellor's analysis in the process. The two options outlined in section B.4.12 quoted above can be seen as presenting a spectrum of possible responses to this issue:

- disguise the client's identity and do not seek the client's permission
- seek the 'informed consent' of your client, verbally or in writing, which implies being clear about what is involved, who will have access to the material and what the purpose of the exercise is
- as above and make whatever is written available to the client

■ as above and include the client's response to what has been
   written in your final submission

Even when the client's consent has been obtained, it is still
advisable to attend to confidentiality by restricting or disguising
information which would lead to identification of the individual. If
you are to share what you write with your client, you will have to
consider the effect on the client of reading very personal information in a disguised form.

An additional aspect when considering confidentiality concerns
the context in which the work takes place. Some agencies and
institutions may have their own guidelines on counsellors reflecting on their client work beyond certain supervision settings. In
these circumstances you will have to check out what, if any, policy
exists and ensure that you operate within any agreed framework.

Apart from confidentiality and client consent, other considerations arise when selecting a client to tape or for a case study, some
of which have ethical implications.

■ If the client's involvement is to be invited, what is your
   assessment of the power balance in the relationship? Is there a
   sufficient level of mutuality for the client to say no? Can you
   ask tentatively enough and accept a negative response? Might
   the person wish to be a 'good' client and say yes simply to
   please you?
■ If the client's involvement is to be invited, what is your assessment of the stage of the therapeutic process? Are feelings
   sufficiently 'owned' to allow reflection? Might your request be
   seen as potentially critical or threatening at this stage in the
   work?
■ In selecting a particular relationship for reflection has the work
   felt difficult/easy, fast/slow? Depending on the length of the
   relationship, will you be overwhelmed with material or will
   there be too little to reflect on? Why would you like to write
   about your work with this particular client?

Developing a coherent, theoretically sound basis for your
position on these issues of confidentiality, consent, the selection of
a client and the degree of client involvement is not only a necessary
starting point for writing about client work but also merits
exploration in the final piece of writing which you produce.

The analysis of a taped counselling session

Many counselling courses require the submission of a tape analysis as part of their assignment programme. The tape may be either audio or video but must be of a good enough technical standard. The box below considers some of the issues about taping. Usually the tape will be accompanied by a transcript and written assignment. As always, read and understand any guidelines which have been issued. You may be asked to transcribe only a certain length of the tape rather than the whole session. Transcribing is a very time-consuming business so it is worth double checking exactly what is required. You may wish to review the tape a few times to select the portion on which to focus if that is what is being asked for. Try and select a period with a variety of interactions – perhaps something that felt difficult or raised questions for you which you will benefit from reflecting upon.

The assignment guidelines may indicate what is expected in terms of 'setting the scene' for this particular session. Clarify how much detail is required on your involvement with this client to date and on the context for this session. A tape analysis is not a case study, so the focus is on giving a background to the session rather than analysing the overall process with this client. Part of 'setting the scene' may include considering the impact of the taping itself on you and your client, including the impact of seeking permission to tape on the relationship. You may also wish to mention any personal circumstances affecting you at the time of this session.

The analysis you are being asked for concerns your experience in the role of counsellor (that is, process). You are not being asked to analyse what your client says in the sense of interpreting or assessing the client's experience (content). You must concentrate on your responses and reactions to the client using your preferred theoretical model to support your analysis.

For example, if your preferred approach is person-centred, you would analyse your responses on the basis of the core conditions, pointing out when you believe you made an empathic response and/or when you stayed within the speaker's frame of reference or slipped out of it. You may recall the sense you felt of acceptance of the client or when that acceptance wavered or disappeared and how this came through in the responses you made. You may examine how you felt at different points in the session and the

---

Issues about taping

Consider how you feel about taping sessions with clients. Explore any reluctance: left unattended, it may affect your efforts.

Seeking the client's agreement or permission
- Think about *when* you will ask for permission – in a first session or when the relationship has been established? How can you ensure that the client is free to refuse?
- What information will you give the client – for example what will the tape be used for (training, supervision) and who will have access to it (tutor, supervisor)?
- Should consent be reconfirmed at the end of the session, depending on the content of the session or the impact of taping itself?
- Notice the effects of taping on both the client and yourself (as counsellor). Was the interaction more guarded? Was there an element of 'playing to the gallery'? Did taping affect the process? Or was the presence of the tape recorder soon forgotten?
- Who owns the tape and/or the contents – client or counsellor? Who will have first access to it? Clients can find the tape of a session useful for their own reflection. (This may surprise trainee counsellors who think of the taping as useful only to themselves.)

Technical Matters
- Tapes *must* be of good technical quality for assessment or supervision. Test the equipment beforehand to check that clearly audible/visible tapes are produced. Check for adequate lighting and reduce background noise as far as possible. Use an external microphone when possible.
- Check (1) recorder, camera, mains socket, plugs, batteries, microphone are all in working order; (2) that everything is plugged in and switched on, volume controls and (where appropriate) contrast and brightness are at the right level, and that the 'pause' button is not left on; (3) that the tape is inserted correctly and is long enough to tape the whole session.
- If technical matters keep going wrong, ask yourself if your anxiety about taping might be manifesting itself. It may be that *you* need attention rather than the equipment.

(see Dryden and Thorne, 1991)

---

extent to which you communicated this to the client. Alternatively, if your theoretical model is psychodynamic, you would identify the particular kinds of intervention you used and relate them to the dynamics operating in the encounter at the time through the transference and counter-transference. You may examine the interpersonal dynamics happening by way of, for example, defence mechanisms and comment on your interventions in the light of these dynamics and your inner experience at the time.

The detailed analysis of exchanges will form the major part of your assignment and should be illustrated by drawing on the actual words, silences and exchanges shown in your transcript. You may wish to comment on any details missed on the tape, for example the visual information not available on audio-tape, or the atmosphere and breathing that may not be picked up on video-tape.

You can round off your analysis by reflecting on the session overall and the impressions you are left with. The following questions may help you reflect on what you have got out of this exercise.

Are you encouraged or discouraged by this piece of work?
Have any themes emerged which require further attention as part of your personal or professional development?
How well do you feel you are integrating theory and practice?

Case study

Counsellors may find themselves writing case studies at various points in their careers: during training, as part of their supervision contract, when applying for accreditation and for research/publication. Whatever the context, the purpose of reflecting on a particular relationship with a client is to show that what is happening in the counselling process can be conceptualised adequately. A case study is an opportunity to demonstrate how theory and practice are integrated. Such pieces of work are not primarily about the client: a detailed description of the client and what has happened session by session would not amount to a case study. Rather the focus will be on the counsellor's experience of the process and the relationship, illustrating a capacity for reflection on, and learning from, the work. The fruits of such reflection will feed back into the work itself and have a beneficial impact: the needs of the counsellor and client meet in the relationship.

As with any assignment, a good starting point is to read and understand any guidelines that are issued by your course. You may be asked to demonstrate the impact of supervision on your work and this may affect your choice of client. The aim of the study may be explicitly to make your way of working with clients visible. This aim may not be met by selecting an unusual or particularly dramatic encounter.

As mentioned earlier in this chapter, there are many issues to bear in mind when selecting a counselling relationship on which you would like to focus when writing about practice. We list these considerations briefly here in the context of doing a case study:

■ the protection of confidentiality
■ the balance between the needs of the counsellor in doing the case study and those of the client in the relationship
■ the extent to which the client will be involved, from seeking consent or not, to asking for the client's input
■ if you wish to invite the client's involvement, the extent to which this is congruent with your assessment of the therapeutic relationship and process. What will you do if they refuse permission?
■ the criteria for selecting a particular relationship. Has the work been difficult/easy, fast/slow, long/short term?
■ the impact your process of reflection may have on the relationship.

Remember the potential for distancing/objectifying the client when writing about practice (see box, p. 132).

There are three elements in a counselling encounter: you, the client and the relationship between you both. You know your experience in the work and your experience of the relationship. You can only know about your client's experience of the work and the relationship in as far as that is communicated to you. The focus of a case study is on what you know and how you conceptualise what you know. In keeping the boundary between you and the client clear, you are maintaining respect for the 'otherness' of the client and lessening the risk of inducing distance between you by the act of reflection.

Outlined in the box below is a suggested structure for a case study. The intention is not to be prescriptive: the shape will vary in every study. The main point to be made is that the bulk of what you write should be focused on your reflection on the counselling process. It can be easy to get carried away with description and detail, but it should be remembered that the purpose of any background information is to set the scene for your reflection on the process and to help the reader understand your reflection in context.

For a useful article, see M. Parker (1995).

Case study structure

Introductory section
1 Your approach to this piece of work. Discuss your stance, and its theoretical basis, regarding confidentiality, consent, the degree of client involvement and the selection of the client.
2 Setting the scene for the reader. Context for counselling (agency, private practice etc.); referral process; contract agreed; length of contact so far – continuing or completed; relevant background information; any involvement with third parties.
3 History of the relationship. Just enough description of the development of the relationship to provide a necessary background for the main section.

Main section
4 Your conceptualisation of your experience with this client. Draw on theory and give references where appropriate. Your experience of the process for the client, for yourself and for the relationship. Draw on your theoretical model regarding issues such as initial assessment, therapeutic strategy, stages in the process and outcome.
5 Highlight any key moments in the process and explore their meaning. Where relevant to your theoretical model, comment on your use of particular techniques/interventions and their effectiveness. Illustrate your personal style and reflect on how well it fits with your theoretical model.
6 Discuss anything you could have done differently. Illustrate your use of supervision if this has been important in this relationship.

Conclusion
7 Reflect on what you have learned from this relationship and from doing the case study. Mention any themes that have emerged for you, indicating areas for future personal/professional development.
8 Consider the relationship and the stage it is at now. State what progress has been made on the client's issues. If the work has been completed, comment on your/your client's evaluation of the outcome.

Key Point

The aim of writing about your practice is to encourage your development as a reflective practitioner who has integrated theory and practice. The focus in such pieces of writing is on you and your work rather than on the client; however attention must be paid to ethical considerations for the protection of your client.

Part III

Continuing to Learn and to Write

14

Beyond the Training Course

In Part III, we explore further the relationship between reading, learning and writing. This involves looking at the connections between thought and language, especially written language, and our perception of reality. Reading is a major learning tool. One of its uses is to collect information, to tap into the 'body of knowledge' in the field of counselling. Through reading, we can also learn more about the human experience. But we can learn more from reading than this: our reading can help us learn how to write. And by continuing to write, we learn more about what we mean, more about how to use language both creatively and correctly and more about how to communicate our learning to others.

Developmental psychologist Jerome Bruner writes that language is important in learning because it gives one 'a way of sorting out one's thoughts about things'. Language itself is part of a culture and the culture provides 'a toolkit of concepts and ideas and theories that permit one to get to higher ground mentally' (Bruner, 1986: 72). Counselling training is contextualised within the culture of counselling, which is already replete with concepts and theories which trainee counsellors meet, come to understand and use in sorting out their own thoughts.

Bruner has said that one of the functions of authors is to make their readers better writers. You can use your reading for a number of purposes. One of these is to gather information, another is to become familiar with the ideas, concepts and theories referred to above. What you read is what someone else has written and this can be an exemplar of how writing should be done: you can learn from and follow the author's punctuation, their use of capital

letters, become familiar with correct spelling and sentence construction. As spoken language can be learned (although only to
some extent) from example and imitation, so can written language.

However, it would be unwise to suspend your critical thinking
abilities as you read. The authors of these texts are also fallible.
Bruner (1986: 57) reminds us of the usual assumption that 'what
others have said must make *some* sense'; even more we assume
that what is *written* must make sense. We also assume that it is
correct syntactically (i.e. is well formed). Neither of these conditions may be true. Therefore, we should not read uncritically; but
as long as we bear that in mind, reading is one of the richest
sources of learning, not only with regard to its content but with
regard to teaching us about writing.

How do you read?

In a collection of essays about reading, the author Robertson
Davies points out that 'vocalising', that is inwardly sounding the
words you are reading, is not usually encouraged (Davies, 1988).
The main reason is that this decreases the speed at which a person
can read. Yet it may be that vocalising passages of reading can lead
to greater understanding and insight into what the author of the
work is trying to convey. Anticipating some of the ideas expressed
in Neuro-Linguistic Programming, Davies asks, 'But how do the
books you read reach your consciousness? By words you hear or
pictures you see? Unless you have a visualising type of mind, by
words. And how do these words reach you?' (Davies, 1988: 15).

Davies's point is that it can be valuable, at times, to sacrifice
some of the speed of reading for greater understanding of particular passages. Not only for simple understanding, but also 'for
pleasure, for emotional and intellectual extension, for the exercise
of the sensibilities'. Try it out: it is worth while using another of
your senses, hearing, in addition to seeing. And if you are someone
who primarily learns through hearing, you may find a great
increase in your comprehension.

After the training course

Most professional counsellor training courses emphasise that the
end of the course is somewhere about the beginning of becoming
a counsellor. As one course puts it: 'It is not to be expected that the

granting of the diploma at the end of the course signifies the end of the process towards becoming a counsellor and developing all the necessary qualities' (PCAI (Hellas), 1994).

What can counsellors do to extend and deepen their learning? In particular, what kinds of reading will help them learn more either about counselling as an enterprise or about the 'raw material' of that enterprise – ourselves, as human beings? There are, to be sure, obvious examples of reading material such as professional journals and the stream (a flood, some might say) of books about counselling, counselling training, supervision and so on. These books, many of which appeal to a popular readership, can be found in any large bookshop and many libraries. The journals may be more difficult to locate outside of a library of a higher education institution which offers counselling training or counselling studies (and not even in all of those). You will find many books on counselling, counselling psychology and psychotherapeutic studies in the catalogues of such libraries. When you are no longer restricted by having to read specific items for your course, it can be exciting to roam through the library catalogue for items that you wish to read out of personal interest.

But it is not only in books about counselling that we can learn about and reflect on what makes human beings the way we are and how our lives may be: a rich source on this subject has always been literature of many kinds, novels, biography, spiritual and religious writing, humorous works, travel books, the arts, sciences, fantasy and so on. A colleague has related (Smith, 1994) that the aforementioned Canadian writer, Robertson Davies, author of books full of psychological insight such as the Booker prize short-listed *What's Bred in the Bone* (1985) was asked how, since he had neither had psychotherapy nor psychotherapy training, he could write 'psychological novels' so convincingly. He replied, 'Why should I need that? I have always considered myself to be well read.' Davies had been turned down as a patient by a Jungian analyst on the ground that he was 'already deeply enmeshed in life' (Grant, 1995).

Contextualising reading: individual and political

Our reading, if it is not confined to counselling texts or to popular writing, can help us bridge the gap between our awareness of individual experience (of discomfort, distress or despair, say) and our awareness of social and political contexts that, in part at least, induce the individual's pain. Moore (1993) uses her knowledge of Romantic poetry (1790–1820) to help her place the counselling enterprise in its political context. The Romantic poets' revolutionary beliefs 'demonstrate how threatening to the established social order it may be to enable individuals, as one does in the counselling relationship, to contact the truth of their own experiencing' (Moore, 1993: 26). The threat is no less today than it was then.

As the client's narrative (the client telling their story) can be considered to be a 'text' which is to be read and understood by the counsellor in collaboration with the client, so that text must be viewed in the light of the social context which produced it. Moore asks us to consider the extent to which 'subjective experiencing' is bound up within the contemporary social and cultural context, and cautions that the client's narrative 'needs to be more fully deconstructed' (Moore, 1993: 34). A fundamental philosophical assumption of a narrative approach to counselling is that 'people live within cultures and construct their identities from the symbols or meanings on offer within their culture' (McLeod, 1996: 178). This is known as 'construction' so that 'deconstruction' is the breaking down or sifting out of the layers of symbolic meaning derived from cultural influences.

A book which explores the political and social context of psychological functioning, *The Political Psyche* (Samuels, 1993) was written, according to its author, to promote a two-way movement from depth psychology into politics and from political analysis and philosophy to the principles and practice of depth psychology. 'It is a question of raising something that is present in culture but unrecognized therein to the more conscious level of a text. If one does that, then the discourse of which that text is a part will be affected by the (new) text' (Samuels, 1993: x). Each time that we are involved in a counselling process, it constitutes not only a therapeutic endeavour serving the client but also an analysis of a text and production of a new text to be added to the social discourse of our time.

In other words, that which we might consider to be an enterprise affecting only the individuals involved (counsellor, client and perhaps their 'significant others') is affected by its social and cultural context and affects this context in turn. This is perhaps most obvious in transcultural counselling (e.g. Lago with Thompson, 1996; Pontoretto, 1995) or in counselling relationships across gender, sexual orientation or social class, all of which are now being given attention in the contemporary counselling literature. Thus, as a counsellor, you are already a co-author of a 'new text' which you may contribute to the prevailing discourse more concretely by writing in the form of reports, articles, reviews, books and so on.

We recognise that some readers may view counselling and counsellors as non-political and may find ideas such as 'social discourse' off-putting. However, as counselling and counsellors come under scrutiny in increasingly challenging and critical ways (see, for example, Howard, 1996) it might be a personal challenge to attempt at least to read some of these more 'difficult' texts. Those interested in this area will find that books such as *Discourses of Counselling* by David Silverman (1996) provide lots of material.

The counselling literature

While you are in training, especially if the course is oriented towards a single theoretical model, it can be distracting and con-fusing to read much in other approaches. Besides, counselling trainees often experience a sense of 'initiation into the tradition' (Purton, 1991: 35) that may lead them to feel disloyal if they read too much from a different tradition. This is more likely to apply to professional counsellor training than to counselling studies courses. However, even as a trainee you may have been encouraged to investigate a counselling tradition other than the core model. After the course it may be both useful and exciting to encounter a different perspective on counselling through widening the scope of your reading.

Classic texts

There are some classic texts in the counselling literature that are well worth reading, even (or perhaps especially) if you do so with a critical approach. We can suggest only a few of those here. Refer to Wilkins (1997: 47) as an example of a source of further suggestions. Any specific suggestions must be, to a large extent, arbitrary. Therefore, in the box below, we mention only a small selection from the so-called 'three forces' in psychotherapy: psychodynamic/psychoanalytic, humanistic/person-centred and cognitive-behavioural.

There is a huge body of literature on psychodynamic approaches. Thus we confine ourselves to the two 'founding fathers', Freud and Jung. Since the 1970s, *The Pelican Freud Library* (Harmondsworth:

Penguin) has published a considerable amount of Freud's writings from the first quarter of this century. Jungian analysis is the subject of a series of books published by Ark paperbacks.

The person-centred approach is represented by Carl Rogers's *Client-Centered Therapy* (1951), and *On Becoming a Person* (1961). A recent compilation of Rogers's writings is *The Carl Rogers Reader* (H. Kirschenbaum and V. Henderson, eds, 1990). Axline's *Dibs: In Search of Self* (1966) is another classic text, endorsed both by client-centred and psychodynamic therapists. Some of the development of client-centred counselling is described in *Innovations in Client-Centered Therapy* (Wexler and Rice, eds, 1974).

A key text in cognitive-behavioural approaches is Aaron Beck's *Cognitive Therapy and the Emotional Disorders* (1976). Principles of a behavioural approach are outlined in (for example) Thoresen and Mahoney's *Behavioral Self-Control* (1974), which can be a mind-opening text for those who consider behaviourism to be little short of a method for imposing one person's will on another.

Modern classics
If anything, it is even more difficult to select from the very large number of books in the current body of counselling literature. However, recent books that should find their way to every counsellor's bookshelves might well include *Handbook of Individual*

Counselling classics old and new

Axline, V. (1966) *Dibs: In Search of Self*. London: Gollancz
Beck, A.T. (1976) *Cognitive Therapy and the Emotional Disorders*. Harmondsworth: Penguin
Dryden, W. (ed.) (1996) *Handbook of Individual Therapy* (3rd edn). London: Sage
Freud, S. (1991) *The Interpretation of Dreams*. Vol. 4, Penguin Freud Library, Harmondsworth: Penguin.
Jung, C.G. (1986) *Analytical Psychology: Its Theory and Practice*. London: Ark
Jung, C.G. (1963) *Memories, Dreams, Reflections*. New York: Pantheon
Kirschenbaum, H. and Henderson, V. (1990) *The Carl Rogers Reader*. London: Constable
Nelson-Jones, R. (1996) *Relating Skills*. London: Cassell
Thoresen, C. and Mahoney, M. (1974) *Behavioral Self-Control*. New York: Holt, Rinehart and Winston
Wexler, D. and Rice, L.N. (eds) (1974) *Innovations in Client-Centred Therapy*. New York: Wiley
Woolfe, R. and Dryden, W. (eds) (1996) *Handbook of Counselling Psychology*. London: Sage.

Therapy (Dryden, ed., 1996), *Handbook of Counselling Psychology* (Woolfe and Dryden, eds, 1996) and Richard Nelson-Jones's *Relating Skills* (1996b).

Biography

Biography can be seen as an interpretation of a person's life, seen through the eyes of one who has researched the 'facts' and commented upon them. Both provide a way to gain experience, albeit vicarious, of lives of persons who may not come into our counselling offices. This is especially useful in the case of those of different racial, ethnic or cultural origins than ourselves; see, for example, Karen Armstrong's *Muhammad: A Biography of the Prophet* (1991). Again, it is important to take into account social and cultural values prevailing at the time in which the biography was written. The exact 'true' story of a person's life can never be told; instead a life story is constructed from and within the meaningful representations of the culture. Consider, for example, the different interpretations of the lives of Cecil Rhodes, Enid Blyton or Bruno Bettelheim.

Biographical works about important people in the history of counselling include the *Key Figures in Counselling* series (SAGE). Biographies of Freud and Jung are readily available (see box below). An interesting development is when real figures are incorporated as characters into works of fiction. This has happened with Freud in, for example, Keith Oatley's *The Case of Emily V* (1993).

Biography – a small selection

Armstrong, K. (1991) *Mohammad: A Biography of the Prophet.* London: Gollancz
Gay, P. (1988) *Freud: A Life for Our Times.* London: Dent
Jacobs, M. (1992) *Sigmund Freud.* London; Sage
Stevens, A. (1991) *On Jung.* Harmondsworth: Penguin
Stewart, I. (1992) *Eric Berne.* London: Sage
Thorne, B. (1992) *Carl Rogers.* London: Sage

Autobiography

Autobiography is an interpretation of the writer's own life. Since autobiographical narratives are often a central feature of the counselling process (McLeod, 1996), it may be useful to counsellors to become familiar with autobiographical writing. Furthermore, a piece of autobiographical writing is often included as part of the written assignment requirements on a counselling training course.

We might imagine that speaking or even writing about one's own life is natural, rather than a product of stylistic convention or cultural influence. However, Bruner and Weisser (1991) have explained how our self-report is bound by strong conventions regarding not only what we say about ourselves, but also how we say it and to whom. These conventions were detected even in the bedtime soliloquies of a child between the ages of two and three years (Bruner and Weisser 1991: 137–41). They show how the text of a life is open to different interpretations by different people (including the person whose life it is) at different times. 'Text' is defined here as 'a conceptually formulated narrative account' which contains a number of recognised narrative markers. Autobiography, or self-report is 'the *first* experience most of us ever have with the crucial difference between a text and its interpretation' (Bruner and Weisser, 1991: 132). When a child gives her account of something that has happened she may sometimes be accused of lying because her interpretation is not the one which a more powerful adult imposes on the event. It is in the light of the reminder that autobiography is a way to 'locate ourselves in the symbolic world of culture' that we must read our own and others' autobiographical writings.

Autobiographical works – a small selection

Abdullah, M.M. (1990) *My Khyber Marriage: Experiences of a Scotswoman as the Wife of a Pathan Chieftain's Son.* London: Octagon

Lessing, D. (1995) *Under my Skin.* London: Flamingo

Mandela, N. (1994) *Long Walk to Freedom.* London: Little, Brown

Mackay Brown, G. (1997) *For the Islands I Sing.* London: John Murray

---

Spiritual and religious writings

Many counsellors (and other people, of course) are interested in the spiritual nature of human beings and the part that religious experience plays in our lives. These days, many who are interested in this area are no longer turning towards orthodox religion or formal religious bodies to provide answers. They do not wish, however, to neglect such an important aspect of being human as spiritual experience represents.

Spiritual works range from translations of ancient traditional texts to modern interpretations of religious experience. Links between the cutting edge of physics (after Einstein and quantum mechanics) and Eastern philosophy, religion and psychology – which in any case are not readily separated – have been made in books like *The Tibetan Book of Living and Dying, The Tao of Physics* (Capra, 1975) and *The Dancing Wu Li Masters* (Zukav, 1979). Both Capra and Zukav comment on ideas about the nature of reality common both to modern science and to ancient metaphysics. For example, the 'in here – out there' illusion: 'What is "out there" apparently depends, in a rigorous mathematical sense as well as a philosophical one, upon what we decide "in here"' (Zukav, 1979: 115). This not only dispels the illusion of 'objectivity' but goes further by stating what has become commonplace in modernity, that an observer cannot observe without altering what is being observed. In the field of psychology, attention is drawn to how perception is dependent on the perceiver and how 'appraisal of threat', say, depends on the belief system of the appraiser interacting with 'out there' stressors (Lazarus, 1976).

Capra (1975: 33ff.) compares 'statements made by scientists and Eastern mystics about their knowledge of the world'. Both of these

---

Books with a spiritual and psychotherapeutic theme

Cooper, H. (ed.) (1989) *Soul Searching: Studies in Judaism and Psychotherapy.* London: SCM Press

Epstein, M. (1996) *Thoughts Without a Thinker: Psychotherapy from a Buddhist Perspective.* London: Duckworth

Feild, R. (1983) *Steps to Freedom.* Putney, Vermont: Threshold Books.

Fox, M. (1983) *Original Blessing.* Santa Fe: Bear and Co.

Fromm, E. (1986) *Psychoanalysis and Zen Buddhism.* London: Unwin

Haeri, Shaykh F. (1987) *The Sufi Way to Self-Unfoldment.* Shaftesbury, Dorset: Zahra/Element

Khan, Pir V.I. (1982) *Introducing Spirituality into Counselling and Psychotherapy.* Lebanon Springs, NY: Omega

Peck, M.S. (1978) *The Road Less Travelled.* London: Simon and Schuster

Thorne, B. (1991) *Person-centred Counselling: Therapeutic and Spiritual Dimensions.* London: Whurr groups distinguish between 'rational' or linear knowledge and 'intuitive' knowledge which 'happens altogether'. Capra points out the connection between rational knowledge, deriving from abstraction and symbolic representation and *writing* itself, which in most languages depicts both language and thought by alphabetic systems of long lines of letters. An exception to this would be *poetic language* which sits somewhere between the language of words and the language of art and music.

More recently, books by Danah Zohar (*The Quantum Self*, 1991) and by Zohar and Ian Marshall (*The Quantum Society*, 1994), 'draw on the many uncanny analogies between quantum reality and the dynamics of self and society' (Zohar and Marshall, 1994: cover).

Fiction

The reflective person can learn from the reading of fiction as well as obtain enjoyment from it. When we asked a number of counsellors what they were reading several of them mentioned escapist fiction. These included science fantasy, someone mentioned the *Disc World* series by Terry Pratchett, detective fiction such as Jonathan Kellerman's *Private Eyes* (1991) and Jonathan Aycliffe's 'ghost story' *The Matrix* (1995). Such reading not only provides escape from the stresses of living but also indicates the capacity of the human imagination and in some way even reflects the enormous range of experience that human life can encompass.

Reading fiction is different from reading counselling texts. Davies (1988) remarks: 'But informative writing requires less effort to assimilate than does fiction because good fiction asks the reader to *feel*' (our italics). Does this surprise you? Perhaps as counsellors or counsellors-in-training we are used to feeling and so do not consider it to be difficult or challenging. The point is that reading fiction which moves us (i.e. elicits emotion) is an experiential process; to get the most from it we need to experience and then reflect on that experience. How many people are prepared to give that commitment to reading a work of fiction?

We are not suggesting that all fiction requires this amount of effort. Yet, every lover of literature will have their own list of works and of authors which make the effort worthwhile for them. The box below lists some more books being read by the counsellors we asked.

Fiction – a small selection

Atwood, M. (1985) *The Handmaid's Tale*. Fawcett Books
Barker, P. (1995) *The Ghost Road*. Harmondsworth: Penguin
Davies, R. (1987) *The Deptford Trilogy*. Harmondsworth: Penguin
Hardy, T. (1985) *Tess of the D'Urbervilles*. Harmondsworth: Penguin Classics
Lessing, D. (1995) *Love, Again*. London: Flamingo
Levi, C. (1982) *Christ Stopped at Eboli*. Harmondsworth: Penguin
Tyler, A. (1996) *Ladder of Years*. London: Vintage

Beware of reading too much

A word of warning should be given here about the danger of reading too much. This applies both to reading fiction and to reading for information or for gaining knowledge from theoretical and other counselling texts. Reading fiction may simply be so enjoyable that it provides a powerful distraction from the hard (and sometimes tedious) work of putting your thoughts into writing.

It is also possible to read too much in preparation for writing a course assignment. This is more likely to happen if your reading is unfocused so that you lose sight of the task itself. Often, the reader then ends up with too much information or material for the essay and may not be able to decide what is to be included or what is to be left out. It can be hard to let go of some of this hard-earned material. When preparing for parts of this book we found a lot of the material so fascinating that it was tempting to follow a trail that led steadily further away from the point of the chapter!

Alternatively, you can read so much that it seems as if everything worth saying has been said already. This can be really deadly when the writing requires a personal voice and original ideas. For example, after writing the bulk of this chapter and the next, we found that some of the same ground is covered in Wilkins (1997). The material fits well into both books and, we believe, is put in ways sufficiently different to be worth saying again. However, if we had read Wilkins's work before writing these chapters it would have been very difficult to find our own voice and we might even have abandoned the chapters on the grounds that it had all been said already. You, the readers, will be the judges of that should you read both books.

Key Point

Reading continues to be a valuable tool for learning about human experience as well as counselling and can help towards becoming a better writer. Each 'text', however (including the 'texts' that clients narrate in counselling), must be considered in its social and cultural context. Different genres of writing all contribute to the store of learning material.

15

Continuing to Write

If you find that you like writing and have some facility for it, you may well want to continue writing after the course is finished. For one thing, you now have the chance to put down all those thoughts and ideas that interested you but which did not fit into the assigned essays on the course. Perhaps you have found a counselling job which entails writing an annual report or contributing to one. Or you are asked to write a book review or to review a training video; or you get notice of a conference and realise that you might be able to write something that fits in with its theme. There are a number of journals to which you could offer an article you have written on a counselling topic about which you have something to say, or perhaps you could begin with a letter to the editor. You may proceed from there to writing a chapter for an edited book and – why not? – to writing a book yourself.

Annual report

An annual report is a cornerstone in any accountability procedure. Counsellors who work in an agency or institutional setting, such as primary health care, a student counselling service in further or higher education, a public counselling service attached to a counselling training centre, an employee assistance programme and so on, will be expected to contribute to, or to produce an annual report. What follows is based on the annual reports of counselling services in universities or higher education institutions. Much can be adapted for other settings.

Two main considerations influence the content of any report: its actual or potential readership and the purpose it is intended to serve.

Readership
Who is going to read this report? The report's readers may include:

■ the governing or regulating body of the institution or agency
■ fund holders or funding body or budget holders
■ other departments within the organisation, sources of referral
■ clients, users of the service, potential users
■ outside agencies with connections to the service

Purpose
The main purpose of the report is usually to *inform*. Information should be given about the counselling work undertaken: presenting problems, statistics about users of the service and other work undertaken (training and development work, for example). The activities of all the workers in the service would be listed: research, publications, further training undertaken, conferences attended (with any papers given), representation or attendance on local, regional and national bodies (counselling organisations and others). The personnel of the service or agency, along with their qualifications and membership of professional organisations, would be listed.

The context of an agency or counselling service will influence the type of issue or presenting problem that brings a client to seek counselling. There is likely to be a high degree of uniformity, at least on the face of it, in the case of specialist agencies such as those offering counselling for survivors of sexual abuse, alcohol problems, bereavement and so on. Generic counselling services, however, need some form of categorisation. The following list is taken from the annual report of a university counselling service.

Central presenting problems at first interview:
■ relationship difficulties
■ depression
■ psychological and emotional
■ anxiety-related
■ bereavement
■ victims of abuse
■ transitions
■ eating disorders
■ physical health/sexual problems

The statistical categories will also relate to the clientele of the agency, but probable divisions will be those of age, gender, referral route, first-time or returning client, whether referred on to another service, how many times seen and, perhaps, some indication of the outcome of counselling. A counselling service in an educational institution will add year of study, mature/non-traditional entry students, overseas students and 'others' – parents/friends of students and, possibly, staff.

As examples, here are the lists of contents for two university counselling service reports:

Report 1
Introductions and reflections on the academic year
Statistics of usage
Staffing
Groupwork
My first few months (for a newly appointed counsellor)
Ancient wisdoms and new approaches in learning
Conferences attended
Development work within the university
Overseas visitors to the counselling service
External invitations
Honorary professional positions held
Publications
The work of the University counselling service

Report 2
The year in the counselling service
Visitors to the counselling service
Leave of absence: travel to South Africa and Australia
One counsellor's perspective on the year
Some reflections on six months with the counselling service (from the locum counsellor while the senior counsellor was on leave of absence)
Training placement
Some statistics
Calendar of activities
Appointments and memberships
Publications
The importance of training and qualification for a professional counselling role.

A report, however, is also a *political* document. It is concerned with the policy and decision-making function of the organisation in which the service is located. The report also has a role to play in educating the organisation (which often has no knowledge of the nature of counselling itself) about counselling and counsellors and their professional status. The box below demonstrates one way in which this educating role was operationalised. In this instance the counselling service wished to counteract the notion then prevailing in certain sectors of the institution that persons without counsellor training could fill the same role as trained counsellors.

An extract from a university counselling service report

Why is training important?
By its very nature counselling deals with people's lives, their psycho-logical adjustment and view of themselves. It touches on areas of mental health: some persons who come to counselling (and can benefit from it) may be quite seriously disturbed. An untrained, unqualified person offering 'counselling' has the potential, therefore, to do a lot of harm. An academic institution would not, rightly, allow mediaeval history (for example) to be taught by an unqualified person; it is even more important that a process that affects not only intellectual development but the development and well-being of the whole person, should not be undertaken in the company of an unqualified counsellor.

Does training by itself guarantee competence?
A successfully completed training goes a long way towards producing a competent practitioner. But counsellors and those experienced in the field (notably the British Association for Counselling) know that con-tinuing professional development is necessary. As well as top-up train-ing, regular consultative support, known as 'supervision', is essential. Thus both individuals and institutions should confirm that the coun-sellors they employ are receiving regular, competent supervision.

A report is likely also to highlight the service's need for resources, to describe how resources are and would be used and to detail the effect of cut-backs on service provision and generally put the case for the service's needs to be met. An annual report is part of the way in which a service fulfils its accountability to the parent organisation. This may require a budgetary statement of how funds have been used. A Statement of Purpose for the service or agency needs to be given (or a reminder of it); this is sometimes called a 'Mission Statement', but the evangelical tone of this title is not to everyone's liking. A Statement of Purpose would include the aims and objectives of the service or agency, along with a development plan for the future. The report may well cover how far the aims have been achieved and the evidence for this.

Writing for publication

Whether or not it is your ambition to be published, it greatly helps your chances of being so if you are known to those who are already writing, editing and publishing material in the field of counselling. This is neither unusual or surprising. Among those who might know you and your writing are course tutors and trainers, colleagues, former colleagues and fellow course members (who may progress to positions of influence with publishers). Once you start writing it is likely that you will be asked again, provided that your writing is of a good standard and that you prove reliable. Other ways of becoming known are volunteering to write reviews and writing letter to editors.

A letter to the editor

Writing a letter to the editor of a counselling magazine or journal or to the editor of a local or national newspaper (on a counselling issue) is one way to begin writing with a view to being published. In such a letter you will be expressing a personal view or opinion which will be informed by your experience, training and/or practice. The letter needs to have some feeling behind it in order to give it some life, but must be properly thought out and backed up by evidence as appropriate.

The letter should be short and concise if it is to have any chance of publication. Letters published in newspapers are generally shorter than those published in journals such as *Counselling*. In any event, editors usually reserve the right to shorten letters. Look in the letters page of the journal or newspaper you are targeting for their policy about letters and how they should be addressed.

It is a good idea to write a draft of your letter without censoring your thoughts, feelings or opinions. Then it is essential to edit the text thoroughly and carefully. Remove the more opinionated passages, especially if you cannot cite evidence for your views, and delete any derogatory (and possibly libellous) references to other people or organisations. If done carefully this does not deprive your letter of its power but adds to its effectiveness. Needless to say it also helps to give your letter a clear structure and to use correct English.

Book review

Writing a review of a book or of another information medium such as a video-tape is a good way of becoming known as a writer – or at least of getting your name in print. *Counselling*, the journal of the British Association for Counselling, is one journal which from time to time invites readers to review books that have been sent in.

As with the other writing projects referred to in this chapter, it is vital to become thoroughly familiar with the format by reading and analysing the book and video reviews published in a number of journals. Do not confine yourself to one journal alone (probably that which espouses your favoured theoretical orientation) but sample the reviews in a number of counselling and psychotherapy publications. Some of these are:

British Journal of Guidance and Counselling
Changes: An International Journal of Psychology and Psychotherapy (Lawrence Erlbaum Associates)
Counselling: The journal of the British Association for Counselling
Psychodynamic Counselling (Routledge)

Contact the book review editor of a particular journal to find out what their policy is on putting books out for review.

Seminar or conference paper

It can greatly help if you become accustomed to presenting a short paper in the setting of a tutorial or seminar on your training course. Not all training courses use this structure; of those which do many are offering training in psychodynamic counselling. A paper presented on a course may become the basis for a paper submitted for publication. Even if there is no formal structure on the course for the presentation of papers, if the written assignments are imaginatively designed, you may have a go at working one of your essays up for a wider distribution.

Presenting a paper at a conference usually takes a certain amount of nerve and courage. Most people find that it does get easier after the first time. Attendance as a participant or ordinary delegate at a few conferences, especially if you listen to the presentations with a critical ear, helps you become familiar with the standard and manner of presentations. You will find that both are very variable.

A paper to be presented at a conference needs to have an element of originality in it. Even if the major part of it consists of material which is already in the literature or otherwise already known, the way in which you present the material, the questions you ask or the conclusions you draw, should be new and arise from your own thinking. You may have done a piece of empirical research and wish to report on it to peers and colleagues, or you may have drawn together threads from the literature either on your preferred approach or on different counselling approaches.

Notice of conferences and 'calls for papers' are advertised in many ways – on training courses and through professional associations (both national and international) and higher educational institutions, for example, and on the Internet. In order to have a paper accepted for presentation at the conference, you will probably first have to submit an 'abstract' of the paper to a selection committee. An abstract is a short (usually about two hundred words) summary of the paper in which the essence of the paper is given, usually along with a note about the author.

The box on p. 162 gives examples of two short abstracts of papers presented at the second and third conferences on Client-centred and Experiential Psychotherapy.

Writing about research

The presentation of a paper at a seminar or conference is part of the process of disseminating research. As McLeod points out, 'we do "research" all the time' (1994: 4). All those engaged in the practice of counselling have immediate experience of the research endeavour. One writer has even described the role of the counsellor as being that of 'research assistant' to the client as researcher into their own personal experience (O'Hara, 1986, cited in MacMillan, 1993). It is a small step from accepting that one is already 'doing research' to seeing oneself as able to take the next step, that of communicating one's research (i.e. one's learning) to interested others. What do you need to do to prepare for this communication? How do you write about what you have learned.

What hypotheses have guided your learning and what new questions or hypotheses has your research generated?

Abstracts of conference papers

Abstract 1

Empathy in Gestalt and person-centred theory and therapy

This study compares empathy as treated in the person-centred approach with empathy as described in the Gestalt literature. After thirty years of stressing the importance of empathy, Rogers (1980) still believed that it needed to be more deeply understood. He believed that too little consideration had been given heretofore to an element which he viewed as extremely important both for the understanding of personality dynamics and for effective changes in behaviour.

In Gestalt therapy the dialogical dimension was specifically noted by Yontef (1980) and Polster and Polster (1973). It would seem that further development of the concept of empathy is possible in both approaches, leading to the conclusion that the ideal is a combination of both.

(O'Leary, 1991)

Abstract 2

Too close for comfort?: levels of intimacy in the counselling relationship

This paper considers the question of intimacy in counselling. Person-centred counsellors/therapists often claim intimacy to be an important ingredient in the counselling relationship, something to be worked towards. As a therapist in private practice, I am concerned to discover more about client perceptions of the therapeutic relationship. Is intimacy something clients strive towards or even want?

The presentation will firstly attempt to give a definition of intimacy within the counselling relationship. It will present findings of questionnaires given to clients over a series of months. The aim will be to explore client perception of the importance of intimacy and whether it is possible to define levels of intimacy which correspond to the needs of individual clients. The paper will then consider my own expectations of intimacy within the counselling process and compare this with the views of other person-centred therapists in Scotland. It will conclude with an evaluation of the impact on the counselling process of differing expectations of intimacy.

(Kilborn, 1994)

As is almost always the case, preparation for writing begins with reading. It is necessary to have a good knowledge of the literature in the area of interest to be able to set your enquiry in context. It is not within the scope of this book to give details of a research study.

A good reference for this is *Doing Counselling Research* by McLeod (1994). Most relevant for our purposes is the section on Writing up Research, especially Box 3.5, 'Suggestions for easing the pain of writing' – one of which reads:

> Writing is a form of thinking. You do not have to have everything worked out before you start writing. The act of writing will help you clarify what you mean. (McLeod, 1994: 41)

Another piece of advice from McLeod is to 'start writing at the very beginning of the project. Keep writing all the way through.' As we have said in previous chapters, it is most important to do this even when the 'project' is a course assignment, and it is essential for a project such as a case study. McLeod (1994: 42) details briefly the process of getting a research project into publication, with particular reference to what are known as 'refereed' journals. A paper submitted to such a journal is sent out to experts in the field for feedback, which is often incorporated into the final version of the paper.

This procedure might well seem very formidable to anyone who is not familiar with it; in any case not everyone wants to work at this level. If you do, it is useful, perhaps necessary, to have a mentor who knows the ropes and who is not awed by the process and those who regulate it, formally or informally. Such a mentor might be a course tutor or director (especially if the course is in an academic institution) or someone with writing and editing experience. The point is that there is little basic difference in the process from that of writing and submitting a course assignment. At whatever level of experience, ask for help and guidance when you need it and do not believe that your work must be absolutely perfect before submitting it for outside scrutiny and feedback.

Other journal articles

Journal articles need not, of course, be research reports. They might focus on some aspect of theory, counselling practice, ethical issue, philosophical background, for example, as well as on research findings. It is likely that an article will draw on several of these areas. The best guide is familiarity with the range of counselling journals and their contents – you should already have got to know some of them on your course.

The journal will carry a description of its purpose and guidance on the kind of articles it seeks to publish. This is usually found at the front or the very back of every copy. For example, the journal *Psychodynamic Counselling* (Routledge) states:

> *Psychodynamic Counselling* is a journal of counselling and consultancy.
>
> The journal will explore the relevance of psychodynamic ideas to different occupational settings. It will emphasize setting and application as well as theory and technique and will focus on four broad areas:
>
> - therapeutic counselling
> - the understanding of organizational and group processes
> - the use of psychodynamic ideas and methods in different occupational settings (for example, education and training, health care, social work, pastoral care, management and consultancy)
> - the understanding of social and cultural issues

The journal will also give guidelines for the submission of articles. These cover:

copyright implications
how articles are reviewed
number of copies to be submitted
number of words for each type of article (full length, shorter length etc.)
presentation of manuscripts
ethical issues, confidentiality, etc.
reference system to be used
additional information – biographical details of author; article details

Although general guidelines are common to most journals, each has its own specific requirements. Therefore check carefully with the particular journal itself: do not assume that you know what they want.

Writing a book chapter

The chances of being asked to write a chapter for a book depends in part on who you know (or who knows you and your interests) as well as what you know and are interested in. With the current huge growth in counselling literature, publishers and editors are likely to be on the lookout for new authors. An edited book may consist entirely of new material or may be made up of material already existing but which has to be adapted for the book. An example of the latter would be a book consisting of the proceedings of a conference. In this case, the editor(s) may well request that the material be adapted to fit the different requirements of a book from a conference paper and (as in other cases) will reserve the right to ask for alterations in the chapter's language and content.

When the book is to be made up of new material, the editor (or editors) ask those who have some expert or specialised knowledge or experience in line with the book's theme. For example, the book *Counselling: Interdisciplinary Perspectives* (Thorne and Dryden, 1993) drew on the experiences and reflections of a number of counsellors who had backgrounds in a range of different disciplines. The editors are likely to supply a common structure or format for each chapter, without, however, squashing the personal style or creativity of the individual writers. The above-mentioned book has sections for each chapter under the headings of:

Introduction
The discipline and my engagement with it
The discipline and my understanding of persons
The discipline and my understanding of the counselling process
Case study material
Conclusion

Common structures for individual chapters can be discerned in many edited books in the counselling literature – see, for example, *Handbook of Individual Therapy* (Dryden, 1996: 395–7).

The main qualities for one who accepts an invitation to write a chapter are commitment, reliability and a willingness to venture into areas which are new and unmapped as far as the new writer is concerned. The ability to keep one's nerve and a fair degree of stamina are also helpful. Writing ability is certainly needed but the help of a good editor can make up for many shortcomings. (For more details, you'd have to ask the editor of this book!) As you submit work in progress, you will learn from the feedback given what are your editor's requirements, likes and dislikes, preferences regarding style and so on, and adapt accordingly. This can be seen as a process of 'shaping'. Remember, however, that you do not have to do everything your editor requests: there is usually room for negotiation.

Writing a book: what does it take?

In answer to this question, perhaps the first essential requirement is a genuine interest in the subject matter. If that is not present, it will be difficult to sustain the commitment throughout the boring, frustrating and seemingly directionless times. Also necessary is the will to complete the work. We have touched on the importance of *will* in Chapters 4 and 12. Interest and will are supported by working out or being given a structure for the book. This is often encapsulated in your book proposal for the publisher or commissioning editor. This is invaluable in terms of keeping the original intention before you and using it as a map should you feel lost at any time. Motivation builds up a momentum as you get going, however, and you may well become quite obsessed with the work, to the point that you resent interruptions from other parts of your life. The transitions between writing time and time for other things may have to be thoughtfully managed.

Key Point

The most important factors in continuing to write are interest in a project and actually producing written material ('keep your hand moving'). Your writing may be for your own satisfaction, as part of an accountability procedure (such as a report), or you may want to communicate research or your views on a particular topic through publishing reviews, articles and even a book. Others do it, why not you?

16

Our Experience of Writing this Book

In this final chapter, we would like to give a taste of how it has been for us during the process of writing this book. One reason is to dispel any notion that we are above all the failings and difficulties that you might be experiencing in the course of your own writing work. We know them, too. The second reason is that, if you are reading this far, then we have written this far, and therefore we have actually made it, we have completed the book. We hope that you can take heart from this.

An earlier version of one of the chapters in this book contained the following story:

> An old woodcarver carved wonderful, lifelike ducks. Someone asked the woodcarver, 'How do you manage to carve such amazing ducks?' 'It's easy,' replied the old person, 'I just find the right piece of wood and then I carve away anything that isn't a duck.'

For us, the story first came up at one of our early meetings in which we discussed the book and how we might go about writing it. We do not know the actual origin of the story but it became one of the strongest metaphors for the process of writing the book.

First, analogous to 'finding the right piece of wood', we had to assemble lots of material (ideas, course brochures, course module descriptors, assessment criteria, readings from relevant texts, examples of written assignments, references, etc.) and then we had to 'cut away' – let go of – all the bits that weren't relevant to the book. One of the problems was that it was very easy to become interested in material that took us off at a tangent, leading us further and further away from the content of the book.

As we neared the end of the writing period, we taped some of our discussions about the process of writing the book. The quotations below come from these tapes.

Beginning

The beginning of the book was a letter from the series editor to one of the authors asking if she'd be interested in writing or co-authoring a book in the Professional Skills for Counselling series. The challenge was hard to resist, so she agreed and asked a colleague if she'd be interested in collaborating on the book.

> *Dot*: There's something fundamental about motivation here. Neither of us have come to a point where we were *driven* to write a book about learning and writing skills for counsellors . . . like, 'This is what I have to say.'
>
> *Mhairi*: Maybe it would have been easier if we had! [*laughter*]
>
> *Dot*: So the question was not '*This* is what I have to say' but '*What* do I have to say?'
>
> *Mhairi*: Exactly. Considering the time when Colin's first letter came – the first tentative enquiry – my response to that was 'Yes, I do have things to say in that area.' But the question that quickly followed on from that was, 'And what are they?'
>
> *Dot*: So they weren't bubbling up . . . they are here somewhere?
>
> *Mhairi*: That's right. So, it required . . . I suppose . . . a certain amount of *faith* that these things would emerge. Part of it has seemed like *extracting*, like drawing teeth almost . . . . At other times, it has been much more like *emerging* – sitting down at the computer and it comes out.

Our beginning, as highlighted in this conversation was very different from that recommended by Wilkins (1997). He suggests that before two people start to write a book together, they should consider:

Who will write what?
How should it be written?
What will be your timetable?
How will information, work-in-progress, etc., be shared?
What will be the process of review?
Who will do the re-writing?
How will you resolve any disagreement?
How will royalties be apportioned?

(Wilkins, 1997: 110–11)

Beyond a tacit agreement that we would probably meet regularly, we did none of these things. We might well have done, if Wilkins's book had been out then, for it is good advice. Perhaps because we knew each other quite well, most of these considerations seem to have been worked out as we went along. Moreover, any initial agreements would almost certainly have fallen by the wayside due to the fact that we both had massive changes in both our professional and personal lives during the course of writing the book. Practicalities were significant: one of us owned a computer and did the bulk of the word-processing work and, logically, the rewriting. One author did most of the writing at first with the other providing ideas and additional material. As circumstances changed, the other author took over the lead in some of the chapters.

Neither of us had access to much secretarial help. It became very clear to us how helpful it would have been to have had an institution behind us which supported our writing as part of our work.

Middle

There was a great deal of 'middle' for the project lasted longer than we anticipated at the beginning. It is important to say here how much one's self-concept can fluctuate during a period of writing. When the work goes well, one experiences oneself as competent and productive: when the work is blocked or progress halted, one can rapidly come to feel unfocused and even become quite ashamed and despairing about the book and think it will never be finished! (Or perhaps this comes from our Presbyterian work ethic backgrounds?) At such times support is invaluable, both from each other and from outside.

At other times, the experience was quite different. Here is another extract from our taped conversation:

> *Dot*: When I was writing the last big chapter . . . things happen on the outside which feed the mulling over . . . that's all I'm saying when I say that I get quite obsessed when I am writing on a particular topic and am immersed in it . . . I think I underestimated the collection of my resources that was required to get engaged at the beginning of the process of writing and then underestimated what was involved in the writing, that it couldn't just be switched off. Somehow that just kept going . . .

> *Mhairi*: That was really unexpected – you didn't expect that you were going to be so much in the momentum, that it would affect you like that, even when you were with a client . . . That's what physical momentum is like, you can't just shut it down because momentum tends to keep whatever is moving, moving . . .
>
> *Dot*: It's also about interest – I tried to mix both [seeing clients and writing] in the same day – *too close for comfort* and I think I recognised it that day.

This led us into talking about the 'inertia' that must be overcome in order to get started and the 'momentum' that builds up and keeps one going to the end of a particular task, after which the inertia has to be overcome again – you can tell that one of us used to teach physics!

> *Dot*: I've felt very energetic in this last wee while about being in the writing . . . I enjoy it, I feel energetic and excited, it has a pay-off it's so easy to forget.
>
> *Mhairi*: I'm thinking about how quickly that can disappear, too, and the task aspect takes over again, especially having finished a chapter and having to gear myself up to do the next bit.
>
> *Dot*: One of the things that struck me was how often you say, 'I was thinking about this as I was walking down to the shops' or your tyre was getting fitted and you had your notebook with you, it [the writing] being with you as you go about your daily activities.
>
> *Mhairi*: Exactly – and I find these wee spaces are very useful because when you are right up close against it you are too close to have the space to sort thoughts out. Things, a whole jumble of stuff, they fall into place, a pattern – *that's* how it can be structured, and then it can get written.

What I learned from writing this book: Mhairi's story

Technical things
I learned many things about using my computer's word-processing capabilities. The only way to learn this, for me, is by using the computer, following the instruction manual when necessary and asking help from one who knows more about it than I do (in my case, my son). I learned how to swap text between my Macintosh and Dot's office PC.

Things about working with a co-author
There were many advantages to working with a co-author. Mainly (and perhaps obviously) was the support given and received in

times of stress, non-production and desperation. We realised that it was inconvenient for us both to be stressed at the same time, since work then proceeded very slowly or not at all. It was very useful to be able to spark ideas off each other and to try out unformed or incomplete notions. It was good also to have someone who would really share the relief and pleasure when things went well.

There were also some features of co-authorship that I found quite hard to get used to. The most obvious is loss of independence. It was not possible to go on my own path without consulting my co-author and allowing myself to be influenced by her views. If you are a very egotistical writer, it is better to go it alone. A related problem is how to handle two voices. Each of us writes with a distinctive 'voice' or style, which might jar or clash if they are not sufficiently blended. One way of handling this might be for the authors to write separate chapters. For many reasons, that was not a suitable solution for us. Partly, it was dealt with by having one of us do the rewriting, but it is not always simple to rewrite someone else's work. At times, I felt we needed to have more contact with each other than was possible, living and working in different locations. At least we were close enough geographically to be able to meet fairly regularly. It was inevitable that we had to go at the pace of whoever was slower at any time. I have had to learn to be more patient with myself as well as others.

Editorial support and guidance

It has been enlightening to observe something of the editorial function in the preparation of a book (which is distinct from preparing a chapter for an edited book). Our editor has been encouraging, prompting us at times, but without putting us under undue pressure, and has guided us by shaping our contributions delicately but clearly and by sending us references to potentially helpful material. Perhaps the most important factor contributing to a successful book-writing enterprise is to choose your editor well! (In fact, it is more likely that the editor will choose you.)

What I learned from writing this book: Dot's story

I enjoy beginnings

My experience of writing this book is that a lot of the inspiration came at the start. I've just dug down through the mountains of paper I've accumulated during the writing process (the size of that mountain is another bit of my learning) and found my notes from the meetings we had when we were planning the book. From agreeing to take on the task, it took about six months to submit a full proposal containing the structure of the book and brief outlines of the chapters. We met regularly over that period, brainstorming and scribbling on flipchart paper on the floor among the tea things. I really enjoyed that stage. We let our minds wander freely, asked big questions, had some meaty discussions and finally came up with a structure which we thought was a sound starting point for the writing.

The energy that gets me into things is not always there when the things need done. It is helpful to me in the middle of the process to refer back to what excited me at the start. This is easier if I've kept a record, in some form, of my excited first reactions to the theme. This process happened, in miniature, with each chapter, even when the final form of what was produced was very different from my initial ideas. It was the act of tapping into that first, fresh energy that seemed to help.

I like writing with other people

Writing need not be a solitary activity. I used to belong to a small creative writing group. We wrote together at monthly meetings, experiencing the power of shared energy in the space we made for ourselves. We never knew what would emerge and my writing thrived when facing the unknown with others. I like writing with companions.

I wrote all my assignments on my counselling diploma course on my own, and Mhairi and I have not produced our writing for this task together. But we have met regularly to swap what we have produced and to discuss where we are and how we are. These meetings have been a vital part of the process. They have served to revive our energy; they have given us short-term deadlines to work towards; they have provided support when we needed it; they have given us space to reflect on our process; they have let us feel less alone with the task. All of that has been much appreciated by me. So there are ways of combining what looks like a solitary activity with support from other people and these ways can be found, whether what is being written is a poem, a book or a course assignment.

Writing a book part-time takes a long time

We are nearing the end of writing this book two and a half years after the initial approaches were made. That is a long time and when I look at what has been produced, I do wonder if it all could have been done much more quickly. But the reality is that a lot of living has been going on alongside this book over that time. There's a parallel here with the difference between doing a full-time or a part-time counselling course. We have been part-time authors and I have had to come to terms with this book being only one part of what I have been living. It has had to find its place among many other aspects of life all jostling for attention. Space has not been cleared for it in the way that I cleared space for my full-time diploma course. The book has not had that level of intense attention. That also means that I've been living with it for so long that I will miss it when it's gone. I am resigning myself to losing a familiar (and demanding!) companion and realise that housework is about to lose a lot of its distracting attractiveness.

Ending

> *Dot*: It has felt like a *long* time, the book's always been there, it's become part of the scenery. I wonder what it will look like when it's not there any more . . . I've never done this before. I had no *way* of knowing what it would be like, it's been like taking on a task and not knowing what would be involved. I've found out that it's not a thing that I've been able to do for an hour or two a day alongside working. I need a lot of energy and focus maintained on it . . . I haven't integrated it into normal life, that's not been possible.
>
> *Mhairi*: It's been like that at times for me. At other times, such as when revising bits, sorting out, cleaning up . . . I can do wee bits at a time. So there's a difference for me between, say, incubating . . . but when it's beginning to come out, it does need a concentrated time without interruptions.
>
> *Dot*: From our last meeting I've written down Colin's comment in response to 'What does it take to write a book?' – something about 'the will to complete', and it's almost like you're saying you got to the stage that you thought it would never be finished and it was at that point that it became 'I *need* to get it finished, I need to get it out of my life.' Which is like creating your own deadline in a way . . .
>
> *Mhairi*: Yes, indeed, yes, it comes from *need*.
>
> *Dot*: Which is not quite what I understand by the will to complete, which I see as something that might be there from the beginning . . . it can feel like forever in the middle . . .

Mhairi: The other thing is, although it'll be great when it's done and out of my life, I'll be sorry if whatever I've learned from doing this didn't get used again. I don't know quite what that is. Maybe it's just learning that it *is* possible.

Dot: I was very aware last time I came, having copied all the chapters up to date, saying, 'This is a book.' But I had the sense that you had seen the outline of the whole more and maybe that does just feel different. You thinking we could do with a bit more here on this and another box there, or change this. And that is a *holding* of the whole in a way that I don't think I've felt.

Mhairi: Yes.

Key Point

There is nothing mysterious or magical about writing a book. The most important factors are commitment, acceptance of delays, re-writing and frustration, and the will to complete on the part of the author(s) and consistent and helpful editorial support.

Appendix

A Summary of Basic Guidelines for Writing Assignments

Note: It is important to consult the guidelines and regulations issued by your particular course, as they may differ in detail from those given here.

Correct English

(1) Sentences. A sentence must contain a subject and a finite verb. This forms a simple sentence with one clause. A compound sentence, which is more common, has one or more subordinate clauses. There is a comma before and after a subordinate clause, as above. A sentence must make sense and have unity of thought. It begins with a capital letter and ends with a full stop.

(2) Paragraphs. A paragraph consists of two or more sentences which share the same unity of thought. A long paragraph may be divided into two, both of which have the same unity. Do not, however, combine short paragraphs into one if they do not have unity of thought. To indicate the beginning of a new paragraph, either:

(i)   miss a line between each paragraph and align the first word with the left margin; or
(ii) indent the first line of the paragraph three spaces, with no line missed.

(3) Syntax. Match verbs with their subjects (singular and plural). Check that tenses are consistent. Use past participles correctly, e.g. 'he has done it' or 'he did it', not 'he done it'.

(4) The correct word. Be precise in your use of words. If you are unsure of the meaning of a word, look it up in a dictionary. The use of a thesaurus helps to find the correct context for the use of a word and provides

synonyms (words with the same meaning) and antonyms (words with opposite meaning).

Language

(1) Use active and passive voice appropriately. There is a difference in the focus of attention between 'I asked my client how he saw the options open to him' and 'the client was asked how he saw the options open to him'.

(2) Avoid using 'he' or 'she' when either he or she is meant. Use 'they', 'he or she' or some other form.

(3) Avoid culture-specific phrases as if they were universal, e.g. 'Christian names', 'Easter holidays'. Instead use 'first names', 'Spring break'.

Punctuation

(1) Capitals. A capital letter is used at the beginning of a sentence and for proper names. The main words in the title of a book are capitalised. Otherwise, use capital letters sparingly. Do not capitalise such words as 'government', 'psychoanalysis', 'psychodynamic', 'person-centred', 'rational emotive', 'counselling' and so on. Refer to usage in a text book if in doubt.

(2) Full stops. A full stop must be used at the end of a sentence. Use full stops after abbreviations, where the end of the word is omitted (Sept., Prof.) but not after contractions, where the middle of the word is omitted Mrs, Dr, eds) or acronyms (BBC, PCA, REBT).

(3) Quotation marks. Use single quotation marks for quoted material in your text. Use double quotation marks for quotes within quotes. Do not use quotation marks indiscriminately to indicate that a word is being used in an unusual sense, such as slang or a technical term or facetiously.

(4) Question marks. A question mark is used at the end of a direct question but not at the end of an indirect question. That is, you would write: This leads me to ask: What are the limitations of this approach to counselling? or: This leads me to ask what the limitations of this approach to counselling are. Use direct questions sparingly in your text.

Numbers

(1) Numerals. Spell out numbers under 100; but use numerals for measurements.

(2) Dates. Follow these formats: 13 January 1905, on 13 January, on the 13th, 1990s (not spelt out, no apostrophe), twentieth century (not 20th century).

(3) Page numbers. Indicate as: pages 154–7, or pp. 154–7, pp. 154–66 and so on.

Style

(1) Clarity. The words you use must say clearly what you mean. Use words with a precise meaning rather than those which are vague. As far as possible, use concrete words rather than abstract.

(2) Brevity. Use no more words than are necessary to express your meaning.

(3) Familiarity. Use familiar words rather than fancy ones, if they express your meaning equally well. However, be prepared to use an unfamiliar word if it is the best or only word for the purpose.

(4) Variety. Avoid repeating the same word in a single sentence. Use a thesaurus to find another word of equivalent meaning.

(5) Do not try to appear clever.

Presentation

(1) All assignments should be typed or word-processed and double-spaced for ease of reading.

(2) Title. State clearly (on the first page or on a cover sheet) your name, the name of your course, the title and/or number of the assignment and the date of submission.

(3) Spelling should be correct and, where there are alternative spellings, consistent. Refer to a good dictionary, such as the Concise Oxford Dictionary. The spell check facility on a word-processor is not always reliable.

(4) Length. Keep to the number of words specified within about ten per cent. More is not better since it does not demonstrate an ability to be selective and concise.

(5) Headings. Use clear headings to mark the start of each section and use sub-headings within each section if needed. A succession of points can be numbered.

(6) Introduction and conclusion. Your introduction should state, briefly and clearly, what you will cover within the essay. Your conclusion should sum up your argument (if relevant) and state your own opinion on the matter. It is not necessary to prove anything.

References

Andriakopoulou, M. (1996) Unpublished essay.

Armstrong, K. (1991) *Mohammad: A Biography of the Prophet*. London: Gollancz.

Assagioli, R. (1974, 1990) *The Act of Will*. Wellingborough: Crucible.

Axline, V.M. (1966) *Dibs: In Search of Self*. London: Gollancz.

Aycliffe, J. (1995) *The Matrix*. London: HarperCollins.

BAC (1996) *Code of Ethics and Practice for Counsellors*. Rugby: British Association for Counselling.

Barwick, N. (1995) 'Pandora's Box: An Investigation of Essay Anxiety in Adolescents'. *Psychodynamic Counselling* 1 (4): 560–75.

BBC Scotland (1991) *One Star in the West: An Interview with George Mackay Brown*.

Bebout, J. (1974) 'It Takes One to Know One: Existential-Rogerian Concepts in Encounter Groups', in D. Wexler and L.N. Rice (eds) *Innovations in Client-Centered Therapy*. New York: Wiley.

Beck, A.P. (1974) 'Phases in the Development of Structure in Therapy and Encounter Groups', in D. Wexler and L.N. Rice (eds) *Innovations in Client-Centered Therapy*. New York: Wiley.

Beck, A.T. (1976) *Cognitive Therapy and the Emotional Disorders*. Harmondsworth: Penguin.

Benson, J.F. (1987) *Working More Creatively with Groups*. London: Hutchison.

Berne, E. (1964) *Games People Play*. Harmondsworth: Penguin.

Berne, E. (1976) 'Away from a Theory', in C.M. Steiner and C. Kerr (eds) *Beyond Games and Scripts*. New York: Ballantine.

Bion, W. (1961) *Experiences in Groups*. London: Tavistock.

Bohart, A. (1993) 'Experiencing: The Basis of Psychotherapy', *J. of Psychotherapy Integration*, 3: 51–7.

Bohart, A. (1996) 'Experiencing, Knowing and Change', in R. Hutterer, G. Pawlowsky, P. Schmid and R. Stipsits (eds) *Client-Centered and Experiential Psychotherapy: A Paradigm in Motion*. Frankfurt: Peter Lang Verlag.

Bondi, L. (1996) Unpublished essay.

Bradford, L.P., Gibb, J. and Benne, K.D. (1964) *T-Group Theory and the Laboratory Method*. New York: Wiley.

Brosnan, M.J. and Davidson, M.J. (1994) 'Computerphobia – Is it a Particularly Female Phenomenon?' *The Psychologist*, Feb. 1994: 73–8.

Bruner, J. (1986) *Actual Minds, Possible Worlds.* Cambridge, MA: Harvard University Press.

Bruner, J. and Weisser, S. (1991) 'The Invention of Self: Autobiography and its Forms', in D.R. Olson and N. Torrance (eds) *Literacy and Orality.* Cambridge: Cambridge University Press.

Buzan, T. (1982) *Use Your Head.* London: BBC Publications.

Capra, F. (1975) *The Tao of Physics.* London: Flamingo.

Casement, P. (1985) *On Learning from the Patient.* London: Tavistock.

Clarkson, P. and Gilbert, M. (1991) 'The Training of Counsellor Trainers and Supervisors', in W. Dryden and B. Thorne (eds) *Training and Supervision for Counselling in Action.* London: Sage.

Collins English Dictionary (1972) Glasgow: Collins.

Combs, A.W. (1989) *A Theory of Therapy.* London: Sage.

Connor, M. (1994) *Training the Counsellor: An Integrative Model.* London: Routledge.

Counselling in Action series (various dates) London: Sage.

Counselling in Practice series (various dates) London: Sage.

Daines, B., Gask, L. and Usherwood, T. (1997) *Medical and Psychiatric Issues for Counsellors.* London: Sage.

Davies, R. (1985) *What's Bred in the Bone.* Harmondsworth: Penguin.

Davies, R. (1988) *A Voice from the Attic: Essays on the Art of Reading* (revised edn). Harmondsworth: Penguin.

Degenhart, D. (1994) Unpublished essay.

van Deurzen-Smith, E. (1984) 'Existential Therapy', in W. Dryden (ed.) *Individual Therapy in Britain.* London: Harper and Row.

Dryden, W. (ed.) (1984) *Individual Therapy in Britain.* London: Harper and Row.

Dryden, W. (1990) *Rational-Emotive Counselling in Action.* London: Sage.

Dryden, W. (ed.) (1996) *Handbook of Individual Therapy.* London: Sage.

Dryden, W. and Feltham, C. (1994) *Developing Counsellor Training.* London: Sage.

Dryden, W., Horton, I. and Mearns, D. (1995) *Issues in Professional Counsellor Training.* London: Cassell.

Dryden, W. and Thorne, B. (eds) (1991) *Training and Supervision for Counselling in Action.* London: Sage.

Egan, G. (1993) *The Skilled Helper* (5th edition). Belmont, CA: Brooks/Cole.

Ellis, A. and Harper, R.A. (1975) *A New Guide to Rational Living.* North Hollywood: Wilshire.

Feild, R. (1985) *Here to Heal.* Shaftesbury, Dorset: Element.

Feltham, C. (1995) *What is Counselling?* London: Sage.

Fewell, J. (1996) Unpublished paper.

Gendlin, E. (1962) *Experiencing and the Creation of Meaning.* New York: Free Press.

Gendlin, E. (1978) *Focusing.* New York: Bantam.

Goldberg, N. (1991) *Wild Mind.* London: Rider.

Gowers, E. (1973) *The Complete Plain Words*, revised by Bruce Fraser (first published 1954)). London: HMSO.

Grant, J.S. (1995) *Robertson Davies: Man of Myth.* Ontario: Viking.

Havelock, E.A. (1986) *The Muse Learns to Write*. New Haven: Yale University Press.

Heron, J. (1988) 'Assessment Revisited', in D. Boud (ed.) *Developing Student Autonomy in Learning*. London: Kogan Page.

Holmes, P., Paul, S. and Pelham, G. (1996) 'A Relational Model of Counselling'. *Counselling*, 7 (3): 229–31.

Honey, P. and Mumford, A. (1986) *The Manual of Learning Styles*. Maidenhead: Honey and Mumford.

Howard, A. (1996) *Challenges to Counselling and Psychotherapy*. Basingstoke and London: Macmillan.

Hutterer, R. (1990) 'Authentic Science: Some Implications of Carl Rogers's Reflections on Science'. *Person-Centered Review*, 5 (1): 57–76.

Inskipp, F. (1996) *Skills Training for Counsellors*. London: Cassell.

Irving, J. and Williams, D. (1996) 'The Role of Group Work in Counsellor Training'. *Counselling*, 7 (2): 137–9.

Jacobs, M. (1988) *Psychodynamic Counselling in Action*. London: Sage.

Jenkins, P. (1995) 'Two Models of Counsellor Training: Becoming a Person or Learning to be a Skilled Helper'. *Counselling*, 6 (3): 203–6.

Jiyu-Kennett, Rev. Master (1989) *Serene Reflection Meditation*. Hexham: Throssel Hole Priory.

Kagan, N. (1984) 'Interpersonal Process Recall: Basic Methods and Recent Research', in D. Larson (ed.) *Teaching Psychological Skills: Models for Giving Psychology Away*. Monterey, CA: Brooks/Cole.

Kellerman, J. (1991) *Private Eyes*. London: Warner.

Khan, Pir V.I. (1982) *Introducing Spirituality into Counselling and Psychotherapy*. Lebanon Springs, NY: Omega.

Kilborn, M. (1994) 'Too Close for Comfort: Levels of Intimacy in the Counselling Relationship'. Paper presented at the Third International Conference on Client-Centred and Experiential Psychotherapy, Gmunden, Austria.

Kirkwood, C. (1990) *Vulgar Eloquence*. Edinburgh: Polygon.

Kirschenbaum, H. and Henderson, V. (eds) (1990) *The Carl Rogers Reader*. London: Constable.

Kolb, D.A. (1984) *Experiential Learning*. Englewood Cliffs, NJ: Prentice-Hall.

Lago, C. (1996) 'Computer Therapeutics'. *Counselling* 7 (4): 287–9.

Lago, C. with Thompson, J. (1996) *Race, Culture and Counselling*. Buckingham: Open University Press.

Lambert, K. (1984) 'Psychodynamic Therapy: The Jungian Approach', in W. Dryden (ed.) *Individual Therapy in Britain*. London: Harper and Row.

Lazarus, R.S. (1976) *Patterns of Adjustment*. Tokyo: McGraw-Hill Kogakusha.

Leitch, H. (1997) Unpublished essay.

Le Shan, L. (1974) *How to Meditate*. Wellingborough: Turnstone Press.

Levant, R.F. and Shlien, J.M. (1984) *Client-Centered Therapy and the Person-Centered Approach*. New York: Praeger.

McLeod, J. (1993) *An Introduction to Counselling*. Buckingham: Open University Press.

McLeod, J. (1994) *Doing Counselling Research*. London: Sage.

McLeod, J. (1996) 'The Emerging Narrative Approach to Counselling and Psychotherapy'. *British Journal of Guidance and Counselling*, 24 (2): 173–84.

McLeod, J. and Wheeler, S. (1995) 'Person-centred and Psychodynamic Counselling: A Dialogue'. *Counselling*, 6 (4): 283–7.

MacMillan, M.I. (1993) 'Education and Counselling', in B. Thorne and W. Dryden (eds) *Counselling: Interdisciplinary Perspectives*. Buckingham: Open University Press.

Masson, J. (1989) *Against Therapy*. London: Fontana.

Mearns, D. (1992) 'Dave Mearns', in W. Dryden (ed.) *Hard-Earned Lessons from Counselling in Action*. London: Sage.

Mearns, D. (1995) *Developing Person-Centred Counselling*. London: Sage.

Mearns, D. and Thorne, B. (1988) *Person-Centred Counselling in Action*. London: Sage.

Meredeen, S. (1988) *Study for Survival and Success*. London: Paul Chapman.

Miller, C. and Swift, K. (1979) *Words and Women*. Harmondsworth: Penguin.

Moore, J. (1993) 'English Literature and Counselling', in B. Thorne and W. Dryden (eds) *Counselling: Interdisciplinary Perspectives*. Buckingham: Open University Press.

Morgan, E. (1972) *The Descent of Woman*. London: Corgi.

Narasimhan, R. (1991) 'Literacy: Its Characterization and Implications', in D.R. Olson and N. Torrance (eds) *Literacy and Orality*. Cambridge: Cambridge University Press.

Nelson-Jones, R. (1984) *Personal Responsibility Counselling and Therapy: An Integrative Approach*. London: Harper and Row.

Nelson-Jones, R. (1991) *Lifeskills: A Handbook*. London: Cassell.

Nelson-Jones, R. (1996a) *Effective Thinking Skills*. London: Cassell.

Nelson-Jones, R. (1996b) *Relating Skills*. London: Cassell.

Neville, B. (1989) *Educating Psyche*. Melbourne: Collins Dove.

Oatley, K. (1980) 'Theories of Personal Learning in Groups', in P.B. Smith (ed.), *Small Groups and Personal Change*. London: Methuen.

Oatley, K. (1993) *The Case of Emily V*. London: Martin Secker and Warburg.

O'Hara, M. (1986) 'Heuristic Enquiry as Psychotherapy'. *Person-Centered Review*, 1 (2): 172–85.

O'Leary, E. (1991) 'Empathy in Gestalt and Person-Centred Theory and Therapy'. Paper presented at the Second International Conference on Client-Centred and Experiential Psychotherapy, Stirling, Scotland.

Parker, M. (1995) 'Practical Approaches: Case Study Writing', *Counselling*, 6 (1): 19–21.

PCAI (Hellas) (1994) *Training Course in Person-Centred Approach Counselling*. Athens: Person-Centred Approach Institute (Hellas).

Perls, F.S., Hefferline, R.F. and Goodman, P. (1951) *Gestalt Therapy: Excitement and Growth in the Human Personality*. New York: Julian Press.

Polster, E. and Polster, M. (1973) *Gestalt Therapy Integrated*. New York: Brunner/Mazel.

Pontoretto, J.G. (ed.) (1995) *Handbook of Multicultural Counselling*. London: Sage.

Pratchett, T. (from 1983) *Disc World* Series. London: Corgi.

Proctor, B. (1991) 'On Being a Trainer', in W. Dryden and B. Thorne (eds) *Training and Supervision for Counselling in Action*. London: Sage.

Purton, C. (1991) 'Selection and Assessment in Counsellor Training Courses', in W. Dryden and B. Thorne (eds) *Training and Supervision for Counselling in Action*. London: Sage.

Rogers, C.R. (1951) *Client-Centered Therapy*. London: Constable.

Rogers, C.R. (1961) *On Becoming a Person*. Boston: Houghton Mifflin.

Rogers, C.R. (1969) *Freedom to Learn*. Columbus, OH: Merrill.

Rogers, C.R. (1977) *On Personal Power: Inner Strength and Its Revolutionary Impact*. London: Constable.

Rogers, C.R. (1980) *A Way of Being*. London: Constable.

Rogers, C.R. (1983) *Freedom to Learn for the 80s*. Columbus, OH: Merrill.

Rowntree, D. (1970) *Learn How to Study*. London: Macdonald.

Samuels, A. (1993) *The Political Psyche*. London: Routledge.

The Scotsman (1996) 13 and 18 September. Edinburgh: Scotsman Publications.

Silverman, D. (1996) *Discourses of Counselling*. London: Sage.

Smith, S. (1994) Personal communication.

Steiner, C.M. and Kerr, C. (eds) (1976) *Beyond Games and Scripts*. New York: Ballantine.

Stones, E. (1966) *An Introduction to Educational Psychology*. London: Methuen.

Swift, K. and Miller, C. (1981) *A Handbook of Non-Sexist Writing*. Harmondsworth: Penguin.

Thoresen, C. and Mahoney, M. (1974) *Behavioral Self-Control*. New York: Holt, Rinehart and Winston.

Thorne, B. and Dryden, W. (eds) (1993) *Counselling: Interdisciplinary Perspectives*. Buckingham: Open University Press.

Toukmanian, S. (1996) 'Clients' Perceptual Processing: An Integration of Research and Practice', in W. Dryden (ed.) *Research in Counselling and Psychotherapy*. London: Sage.

Watzlawick, P., Weakland, J. and Fisch, R. (1974) *Change*. New York: Norton.

Wexler, D. and Rice, L.N. (eds) (1974) *Innovations in Client-Centered Therapy*. New York: Wiley.

Wheeler, S. (1994) 'Counsellor Training – Choosing the Right Course', *Counselling*, 5 (3): 210–12.

Wheeler, S. (1996) *Training Counsellors: the Assessment of Competence*. London: Cassell.

Wilkins, P. (1997) *Personal and Professional Development for Counsellors*. London: Sage.

Woolfe, R. and Dryden, W. (eds) (1996) *Handbook of Counselling Psychology*. London: Sage.

Yontef, G.M. (1980) *Gestalt Therapy: a Dialogic Approach*. Unpublished.

Zohar, D. (1991) *The Quantum Self*. London: Flamingo.

Zohar, D. and Marshall, I. (1994) *The Quantum Society*. London: Flamingo.

Zukav, G. (1979) *The Dancing Wu Li Masters*. London: Rider.

Index